The Ultimate Guide To Careers In Aviation

Julien Martinson

© 2024 by Julien Martinson

All rights reserved. No part of this publication may be reproduced, distributed, or transmitted in any form or by any means, including photocopying, recording, or other electronic or mechanical methods, without the prior written permission of the author, except in the case of brief quotations embodied in critical reviews and certain other non-commercial uses permitted by copyright law.

First Edition

Library of Congress Cataloging-in-Publication Data

Names: Martinson, Julien, author.
Title: The Ultimate Guide to Careers in Aviation / Julien Martinson.
Description: First edition. | Toronto: 2024. | Includes bibliographical references and index.
Identifiers: ISBN 979-8-9903768-0-9

Cover design by Kyle Ryan
Book layout by Joel Mark Harris
Printed in the United States of America by Kindle Direct Publishing

The information in this book is meant to supplement, not replace, proper aviation career training. Like any other field of activity, aviation careers require specific qualifications, credentials, and expertise. Always seek the advice of professionals. For more information, visit https://www.julienmartinson.com

Dedicated to the passionate individuals who work tirelessly behind the scenes to keep the wheels of aviation turning. Your dedication and commitment ensure that the dream of flight remains a reality for all who dare to soar. As special thanks to my mother, Tessy Kessler and my father, Wilfried Haest who have supported me in passion for aviation and continuously to dream bigger.

In addition, a thank you to my aunt, Rita Matthys Tavernier for encouraging me to pursue my dream to inspire other with financial support. And Joel Harris for his editorial assistance to make this book take off. Finally, to the next generation of passionate aviators, who will take the aviation industry to a whole new level.

Table of Contents

Preface …………………………………………..5

Introduction……………………………………7

An Overview of Aviation………………………….14

Aviation By Region……………………………..24

The World of Airports …………………………..35

The Role of Airlines……………………………..50

A Good Career Path…………………………..64

The Role Of Commerce In Flight…………………76

Pilot Careers……………………………………..93

Air Traffic Control………………………………107

Venturing Into Aircraft Engineering …………….118

Aviation Management…………………………..131

How To Find A Job In Aviation………………….148

The Future Of Aviation…………………………156

Preface

Welcome aboard,

As I sit down to write this preface, I'm reminded of the countless times I've gazed up at the sky, feeling a surge of exhilaration as planes streaked across the horizon, each one a testament to human ingenuity and the boundless possibilities of flight. It's this awe-inspiring sense of wonder that has fueled my own passion for aviation, propelling me through the highs and lows of a career in this dynamic industry.

But before we soar into the pages ahead, allow me to introduce myself. My name is Julien Martinson, and aviation isn't just a profession for me—it's a lifelong fascination that has shaped my journey from the start of my career to becoming an industry expert. With over 25 years of experience in the aviation industry and entrepreneurship, I've had the privilege of witnessing first hand the transformative power of aviation and the diverse array of careers it encompasses.

The purpose of this book is simple yet profound: to serve as your trusted guide on the flight path to a rewarding career in aviation. Whether you're a wide-eyed enthusiast dreaming of taking to the skies or a seasoned professional seeking new opportunities, this book is designed to equip you with the knowledge, insights, and inspiration you need to navigate the complexities of launching a career in the aviation industry with confidence and clarity.

Throughout the chapters that follow, I invite you to embark with me on a comprehensive exploration of aviation careers, from the cockpit to the control tower, from the hangar to the executive suite. Drawing on my own experiences and those of industry luminaries, together we will delve into the intricacies of each career path, uncovering the skills, qualifications, and opportunities that await aspiring aviators like yourself.

But this book isn't just about facts and figures—it's about passion, perseverance, and the unwavering belief that the sky is not the limit, but the beginning of endless possibilities. It's about embracing challenges, seizing opportunities, and charting a course that honors your unique talents and aspirations.

So, dear reader, I invite you to buckle up and prepare for takeoff. Whether you're embarking on your maiden voyage or navigating a career crosswind, know that you're not alone. Together, let's soar to new heights and discover the extraordinary world of aviation careers.

Clear skies and tailwinds,

Julien Martinson

Introduction

Ever since our ancestors looked up at the sky, we have wanted to master it. And, today, in the 21st century, we often take travelling by airplane for granted. Travelling across the world used to take weeks, months, and even years, but now you can go to any country in the world in a single day. If one were to jump on a flight from Los Angeles to Beijing, it would take 14 hours and 40 minutes. From Vancouver to Timbuktu takes even less time—13 hours. Remarkable, isn't it?

A hundred years ago, if you were European, you had to board an ocean liner from Liverpool or Hamburg, and it would take you a week or even longer to get to New York. Forget if you want to travel elsewhere in the United States, like the Midwest or California. Before the Industrial Revolution, and the invention of the steam train in the latter half of the 1700s, travelling across land wasn't only time-consuming, but, oftentimes, it would be dangerous.

Then air travel was invented, and travel has never quite been the same since. Just think—a couple of generations ago, it wasn't that uncommon for a person not to have left their home city—let alone their home country. Now it's almost impossible not to meet someone who has done, at least, some travelling in their lifetime. Today, air travel has never been so affordable or so easy.

When you look closely at aviation, it's easy to see how it stands apart from any other industry. The aviation industry is also deeply tied to country sovereignty and national pride. For example, every aircraft, whether military or civilian, is registered in a specific country, and this registration serves as the aircraft's legal nationality. Unless you are an aviation aficionado like myself, you probably didn't know that this was decided on at the International Air Navigation Convention held in 1919. For civilian aircraft, this registration process is just like the license plate system used for automobiles. Each country has a unique one or two-letter prefix to designate its registered aircraft. For example, aircraft registered in the United States begin with the letter 'N'; in Canada, unsurprisingly, it is a 'C'; while in the United Kingdom, their designation starts with 'G'.

Upon registration, the aircraft is given a unique combination of letters and/or numbers that follow the country's prefix, collectively known as the aircraft's tail number or registration mark. This allows for the easy identification of the aircraft's country of origin and its individual identity. The registration is essential for various administrative, operational, and legal reasons, including ensuring safety compliance, tracking aircraft movements, and establishing ownership.

Military aircraft, on the other hand, are registered and numbered according to each country's defence protocols. Each country's registration is a little different, but generally, they typically have their own set of unique identifiers, often reflecting the type, role, or unit of the aircraft. However, there is no international registration or governing body that oversees military aircraft as there is with civilian registration.

I have been fascinated by air travel ever since I was a little boy when I went on my first trip from Vancouver to Charlottetown. It was a long flight – around 8 hours – and I must have driven the poor flight attendant crazy, asking her a thousand questions about how the plane was kept in the air, how the pilot controlled the plane, and how the navigation worked. The flight attendant patiently answered my questions as best as she could. I would stare out the window at the puffy white clouds and blue sky, amazed at the beauty that surrounded us. Like an addict, I became hooked.

As I grew up, I quickly realized that the aviation industry has a unique history that started with the Wright Brothers when manned flight was only an idea. It didn't take long for entrepreneurs to see the potential. The first airline in the world was a government-sponsored company, DELAG, which was founded just one year after the Kitty Hawk flew across a beach in North Carolina. In 1914, the world's first passenger service set off from St. Petersburg, Florida and landed in Tampa. The airline only ran for four months, but it unlocked a world of possibility.

United Airlines became a powerhouse in the industry when a combination of airlines merged with each other in the 1930s. In my home country, Air Canada was founded after the federal government's 1936 creation of the

Trans-Canada Air Lines. All major countries –whether it's England, France, Germany, China, or Brazil have national airlines. These airlines are a symbol of national sovereignty. While most of us have a love/hate relationship with our national carriers (who hasn't complained about their national airline on social media?), they stand as a testament to what makes each of our countries special and unique. I, for one, can't imagine life without Air Canada. It has taken me across the world and allowed me to experience different people and their cultures—something I am forever grateful for.

Let's turn to air sovereignty, an important concept in aviation. Land and water sovereignty have been concepts that have been around for thousands of years. However, the idea of air sovereignty has never been an issue, primarily because up to about a hundred years ago, someone couldn't invade or attack another country from the air. Today, we don't think much of it: The sky above a country belongs to that country. When a foreign air balloon crossed over into the United States early 2023, it was perceived as an incursion onto American sovereignty.

Unfortunately, with modern technology, bombs and missiles can easily kill from above, and often they do, but looking back at human history, air sovereignty is a relatively new concept. Today, there are military organizations that have only one job: To protect our skies. In North America, there is NORAD (North America Aerospace Defence Command), which was founded after World War 2 when Russia started to build up their military. Long-range bombers, cruise missiles, and, of course, the atomic bomb became very real possibilities and had to be defended against.

National pride is just one reason why aviation is so different from other types of industries. When aviation first started, countries competed with each other to be first to cross the English Channel or the Atlantic Ocean, or to be the first to transport goods across a continent. There is something intangible about flight that gives us a different perspective, even a different outlook on life. There is no better place, in my mind, to do some serious contemplating than at 35,000 feet above the Earth, hurdling many miles per hour. Looking through the clouds, sometimes catching a glimpse of the Earth below, can really help shift your perspective. For me, it's the equivalent of climbing up the mountain to speak to the wise man.

Aboard an aircraft, one can truly grasp the magnitude of who we really are and what matters.

Then there is aviation's version of groupies—called plane spotters. To an ordinary observer, the outskirts of an airport might seem an odd place for enthusiasts to gather. Armed with cameras, binoculars, and often, logbooks, these individuals can be seen dotting the airport perimeters, eyes glued to the skies or the runways, eagerly awaiting the next landing or take-off. What other industry has the dedication of such hardcore fans? There is just something about an airplane cutting through the air–the way it looks, the angles, the curves, the sound of the engine all attract attention.

In west-central Wales, there's a series of valleys named the March Loop which is famous in the airplane-watching community because military planes practice their low-flying abilities there. Pilots from all around the world use the March Loop for practice and spotters use it as an opportunity to watch, photograph, and record these magnificent airplanes which are marvels of modern technology. You can see F-15 Eagles, F-16 Fighting Falcons, F-35 Lightning II, the Eurofighter Typhoon, as well as bigger aircraft like the C-130, and the A400M. I urge you to search the March Loop on YouTube! There are tons of incredible videos that have been posted for your enjoyment and you can easily spend hours going down the rabbit hole.

The origins of modern-day airplane spotting trace back to wartime Britain when spotters were initially civilians trained to identify enemy aircraft during World War II. Their observations aided in defense efforts, alerting communities and military personnel about potential threats. But of course, people watched airplanes since the Wright Brothers first took flight!

I would be amiss if I didn't mention the importance of national defence in the advancement of aviation. During WWI and WWII, aircraft were not just marvels of engineering but also symbols of might, as the allied and axes countries raced in a battle for the skies. At first, airplanes were used solely for reconnaissance, but as they became more sophisticated, the planes were fitted with bombs and machine guns to attack ground troops. These planes would run into enemy planes trying to do the same thing, and dogfighting was invented. War accelerated aviation technology with inventions such as the closed cockpit, the all-metal fuselage, and the pressurized cabin.

When Top Gun came out in 1986, it famously tapped into many young men's fascination with fighter jets. Famously, the movie led to a 500 percent increase in Navy recruitment—whether that is true or not, we cannot really know. Of course, what is true is that the film focused on the Navy and increased public awareness of careers in the military. But people also became aware that there was a whole world of aviation—people didn't just have to become fighter pilots; they could fly commercial jets, fix aircrafts, and become air traffic controllers.

According to the International Council of Air Shows, an average of 340 air shows take place every year in the United States and Canada. These are huge productions that bring planes and pilots from over the world to perform, maneuver, and show off for thousands of people. The Paris Air Show is the largest in the world, with approximately 300,000 visitors and 2,5000 exhibitors from 46 countries, and a display of 150 aircraft. I was lucky enough to visit the Paris Air Show in July 2023. It was only the second year after it had been cancelled because of COVID, and I was overwhelmed by the sheer number of people all packed into one place. In fact, I have never seen so many aviation trade suppliers under one roof.

Beyond military applications, the aviation industry also changed how mail was delivered. Today it's something that most people take for granted, but it was a significant leap forward. Not many people know, but apart from transportation and military reconnaissance, delivering mail was one of the earliest applications for planes. A man named Fred Wiseman was the first unofficial mail carrier when he took three letters from Petaluma to Santa Rose in California in 1911. Perhaps, surprisingly, the first official airmail flight was organized by Sir Walter Windham in India when a service was created to generate publicly and raise money for charity. Sir Windham then went home to London and performed the first scheduled airmail post service in the U.K. as part of King George V's coronation. The first official American airmail delivery was completed by the United States Post Office on September 23rd, 1911, seven months after Wiseman's flight.

For the first half of the 20th century, airmail and surface mail were sold as separate services, and people often had to go to different companies based on whether they wanted their mail to go by land or by air. Today, airmail is integrated into other types of mail services and performed by companies like FedEx, DHL, and Amazon, allowing us to ship things overnight faster than ever before. While letters aren't perhaps as common as they once were, people still feel excitement when they receive them, especially when they have the special 'Par Avion' sticker or label, which literally means 'by airplane'. Why are the stickers written in French? Good question! The Universal Postal Union, which was established in 1874 in Switzerland, adopted comprehensive rules for airmail at the Postal Union Congress in 1929. And since the Postal Union's language is French, 'Par Avion' was designated as the official stamp denoting the mail arrived by mail, usually also meaning it is first class.

There is something special about receiving a letter or parcel with 'Par Avion' written on it. It means the mail is important and that the sender took extra care and spent more money for you to get it. Can you remember the last piece of mail you received that was sent by air? It stands out from the other types of mail—which, if we are being honest—are mostly junk mail these days. Shifting through your mail, most people stop when they see the sticker. The envelope is usually different too. Sometimes it's thicker, usually, the address is handwritten in blue or black ink. While the 'Par Avion' sticker is something of a fading tradition, it still helps family and loved ones across the world connect.

This brings me to the airports, which are mini-cities amongst themselves, whole complex ecosystems. Airports, for many travellers, are the beginning of new adventures and experiences. They stand as the gateways to nations, often leaving lasting impressions on visitors from far-off lands. In essence, airports are more than mere points of departure or arrival. Through their halls, runways, and services, they echo the aspirations of nations and stand as monuments to human achievement and dreams for tomorrow. There is much we can say about airports, and we will delve deeper in later chapters, but I think it's important that I touch on them here.

The airports, however, wouldn't be anything without the actual airplanes and the airliners.

The airlines play pivotal roles that ripple outwards through global economies. Direct employment, from ground staff to aircrew, to the duty free shops, and, of course, the tourism that floods out into the cities as a whole.

This book aims to capture the importance of the aviation industry as a whole, not just for those who are directly employed but also indirectly. In truth, the aviation industry plays a part in all of our lives. Whether we benefit economically or not, we HAVE benefited from the technology.

I hope to establish that the aviation industry is a great career for those who are motivated, dedicated and passionate about the skies. And ultimately, how they can best fit in with the job that best suits the individual. Of course, aviation is not for everyone—it certainly takes a certain personality; in most cases, an adventurous spirit doesn't hurt. But I'm guessing if you picked up this book, then you feel the allure of flight.

I've split this book up by first, giving the reader an overview of aviation and what it's like to work in the field. But then I dive into the different fields: pilots, aviation engineers, air traffic controllers, and aviation management. I purposely left out careers like flight attendants, baggage handlers, and customer service representatives, not because they are any less important to the smooth running of air travel, but because they take different skillsets and are generally easier to get hired in. While I would love to write about flight attendants, you don't need a book in order to get hired on as one.

I spent many years desperately wanting to get into the industry, but not fully understanding my options. I knew that one could become a pilot, of course, but later in life I discovered there are many different paths to take. If I had read a book like this in my earlier years, then I'm sure my life would have taken a very different turn. Most likely, I would have gone into management at a company like Air Canada, but I didn't have a mentor or anybody to guide me. I hope that this book will be the starting point for you.

Lastly, I hope that I am able for potential candidates to go into aviation with eyes wide open. Like any industry, it's not without its problems. And like many skilled jobs, as more people in the aviation industry reach retirement age, there is a shortage of qualified professionals. While many industries are worried about machines taking over, those going into the aviation industry, for the most part, are safe. Unlike taxi drivers and long-haul truckers, who have to worry about self-driving cars, AI isn't going to pilot an airplane any time soon. Machines might make scheduling and engineering manufacturing more efficient, but there still needs to be more human oversight—more so than in any other industry, and that is just one aspect that makes aviation so unique.

So read this book with an open mind and if you need any help or assistance, please don't hesitate to reach out by visiting my website julienmartinson.com.

Chapter 1:
An Overview of Aviation

I've flown around the world, and the Vancouver International Airport has always been the apple of my eye. The engineers, architects, and designers did an incredible job incorporating aboriginal traditions, nature, and simplicity into the decor. I get goosebumps just thinking about it—every time you exit the international gate, you walk over a gangway, and you see this stunning waterfall, and then just a little further, you are greeted by a bronze-cast statue that was created by the famous Canadian artist Bill Reid called: "The Spirit of Haida Gwaii," a beautiful piece of artwork that incapsulates the Pacific West Coast so perfectly. After a long and probably stressful flight, your surroundings can help you feel relaxed and at peace. First impressions are important, and if airports are done right, they should represent their city, their country, and the region's history. The Vancouver International Airport does this perfectly.

But an airport is much more than just the look and feel of the building when you arrive. They are like large, complex machines with all types of gears, levers, and running parts, working together. Airports have been described as cities within a city, and, although it's become a bit of a cliché, there's reason for the comparison. Airports are cities on to themselves. They have their own police forces, fire departments, paramedics, garbage attendants, and miscellaneous support staff. One could very well live in an airport and want for nothing, as demonstrated in Steven Spielberg's movie 'The Terminal.'

In recent years, airports, like other organizations, have been trying to find ways to cut down on their carbon footprint and become more environmentally sustainable. One promising solution is refining Air Traffic Management, which, by optimizing flight paths and airport operations, can lead to significant reductions in fuel consumption, greenhouse emissions, and noise disturbances.

In Toronto Pearson's airport, they have a program called YYbeeZ (yes, that's really what it's called) where there are 15 beehives and close to a million bees which are kept on the airport premises. The honey from the bees is then sold at the airport. This was just one initiative that allowed Pearson to be the first airport in the world to achieve the highest level of environmental management.

Also embracing the farm-to-table trend is JFK's JetBlue Terminal. There, local farmers are growing their own produce, bringing fresh, local, and sustainable food options straight to the traveller's table from its 24,000-square-foot garden. Not only does it provide travellers with fresh, local ingredients, but it also brings awareness to the importance of environmental sustainability.

Other airports opt for a more direct approach. Singapore's Changi Airport stands out with its solar-powered terminal, while the Denver International Airport captures attention with its expansive on-site solar farm. By dramatically reducing their carbon footprints, Singapore and Denver are not just saving on energy costs, they're investing in the future of renewable energy for generations to come, inspiring airports around the world to reimagine their relationship with the earth's resources.

Auckland International and Chicago O'Hare are going green in a more literal sense. They've infused their terminals with vertical gardens and lush green spaces, which not only purify the air and reduce traveller stress but also elevate the aesthetic ambience of bustling terminals.

However, going green is more than just planting a few vegetables or installing some solar panels. The balance lies in ensuring airports can take on additional traffic while also being aware of their environmental footprint. This is especially critical given that airports significantly boost both local and national economies by facilitating trade, tourism, and employment.

Programs are also – to be frank – good PR opportunities. It is important to keep municipalities, governments, and local communities happy as they often have a say in the future of airports, and whether they can expand or not. If an airport does not take into account the needs of people who are impacted by the airport, then opposition can form, and it can hinder development.

So, what should decision-makers do to increase sustainability? Apart from the aforementioned options, there are a few directions airports can take. They can prioritize and promote environmental sustainability by drafting and implementing national regulations tailored to the needs of airports. An inclusive approach that ensures local communities and various stakeholders are involved in airport development can foster more holistic decisions, likely reducing potential opposition.

There are other types of innovation that go beyond just environmental. Airports like Abu Dhabi International, Mexico City International Airport, and Tokyo's Hanea are introducing unique solutions such as sleep pods, mini-hotel rooms, full-service restaurants that cater towards travellers who have particularly long layovers. Apart from bringing in more revenue for the airports, these solutions can make travel easier and more enjoyable.

And to better address a traveller's physical and mental well-being needs, airports, such as Baltimore-Washington International and Dallas/Fort Worth, have integrated yoga rooms, walking paths, and full-scale gyms. Now, passengers can stretch, meditate, or even break a sweat between their flights. In these airports, a traveller can find serene yoga rooms amidst the hustle and bustle. Here, one can unroll a yoga mat, strike a pose, and find a moment of zen before the next leg of their journey.

Airports are also becoming cultural hubs that extend beyond the traditional role airports usually have. For example, a stop at Seoul's Incheon Airport might surprise travellers with traditional Korean cultural performances and craft activities, ensuring visitors get a dash of Korean culture without stepping outside the airport.

Technology Advancements in Airports

Unsurprisingly, technology plays a big part in increasing airport efficiency and passenger enjoyment. TechDubai International Airport has streamlined its boarding processes with biometric self-boarding gates, while many other airports, especially in a post-pandemic world, are introducing touchless check-in kiosks to enhance passenger experience and safety.

In the bustling hubs of our airports, every passenger, every flight, every movement is a story told through data. This data is a treasure trove of information on passenger flows, flight schedules, and the intricate details of day-to-day airport operations which can be utilized into a roadmap to improve airports. This practice is known as data mining and can provide an overall experience that's not only smoother but also more reliable.

For instance, data revealing consistent crowding in certain areas might lead to the opening of additional lanes or redirection of foot traffic. Additionally, the management of flight schedules and gate assignments can be optimized by examining data on arrivals, departures, and gate usage. This approach minimizes delays and maximizes gate and runway utilization.

Predictive maintenance becomes more streamlined through the analysis of data, preventing breakdowns and ensuring smoother operations. Efficient resource allocation is another key area. For example, real-time data analysis aids in deploying staff, security, baggage handlers, and shuttle services to the right areas of the airport. Airports can also enhance the passenger experience by personalizing services based on data on preferences and behaviors, offering tailored retail and dining suggestions or customized travel information via mobile apps.

Data on passenger demographics and spending habits assists airports and retail partners in maximizing revenue through optimized offerings. Managing increased passenger loads during holidays and peak travel times becomes more efficient with data-driven crowd management strategies. Finally, long-term strategic planning, such as terminal expansions or investments in new technologies, is informed by the accumulation of data, allowing airports to adapt to evolving passenger needs and trends.

Then there is Virtual and Augmented Reality (VR and AR) which is another change aviation. In the next couple of years, this market has the potential to be more than just gimmicks—they can be powerful tools reshaping training, maintenance, and safety in aviation. VR and AR offer an immersive world, linking the digital and physical realms of the aviation ecosystem, leading to streamlined operations and cost savings.

For example, when it comes to maintenance, these technologies can revolutionize procedures. AR can assist maintenance personnel by displaying real-time information and 3D diagrams over physical components of the aircraft. This can significantly reduce the time and potential errors in diagnosing and repairing aircraft, leading to increased efficiency and reduced downtime for maintenance.

In terms of safety, both VR and AR can contribute significantly. VR can be used for emergency response training, allowing crew members to practice procedures in highly realistic, simulated environments. This prepares them better for real-life emergencies. AR can enhance safety by providing real-time information to pilots and ground staff, such as navigation paths on runways or critical flight data, reducing the likelihood of accidents.

But beyond operational efficiency, AR and VR are poised to redefine passenger experiences. Lufthansa's trial with Avegant's Glyph, a world leader in AR and VR, has shown promise on how this technology might serve passengers. Guests visiting Lufthansa's Business Lounge at Frankfurt Airport could test Avegant Glyph video glasses, which provided users with a personal cinema experience, video conferences, or gaming. The video glasses could be connected to smartphones, laptops or gaming consoles via a micro-HDMI cable for a variety of uses. Next LEDs projected the video signal onto two fields, each of which have tiny, microscopic mirrors. Lenses then focus the light reflection and cast them onto the viewer's retinas.

The trial of the Avegant Glyph video glasses followed a recent test of VR headset at a departure gate at Frankfurt Airport. Economy class passengers were given the opportunity to use the VR headset to explore the Premium Economy cabin. Following the immersive experience, they were given the option of upgrading to a Premium Economy seat for a fee. These trail cases not only offer passengers a unique experience but can also be used to help airline companies upsell their customers.

As we look to the future, we can expect more airlines and airports to collaborate, leveraging these technologies not just for operations, but also to engage passengers, and increasing the amount of money passengers spend—a win-win for airports and airliners alike.

The Growth of Aviation

With everything that goes on in an airport, it should come as no surprise to discover that aviation is big business. According to Statistica, the global market size of the aviation industry is worth a staggering $841.5 billion, which is a seven percent increase over last year. Since 2020, aviation's worst year in recent memory, hiring has increased by 32 percent across the board, according to the U.S. Transportation Board.

With many in the aviation industry looking at retiring, airlines are on a massive hiring spree. Never has there been a better time to get into aviation. United Airlines, one of the world's biggest airlines, plans to hire 50,000 workers by 2026, which will add to their already-strong 93,000 workforce. Southwest Airlines plans to hire 7,000 in the next few years and while Delta Airlines hasn't made their projections public, they have already hired 20,000 workers since the start of 2021.

So what is fuelling the growth of the aviation industry? For starters, there has been the recovery from COVID. Unsurprisingly, the aviation industry was hit hard, and now that the pandemic is firmly in the rear-view mirror, people want to travel more, and we shouldn't expect this to change in the foreseeable future.

However, ultimately COVID is just a blip on the radar. The aviation industry has been growing, and in some cases, exponentially. These are the more important factors because they are the long-term factors that will shape aviation in the decades to come.

Air travel, once a luxury for the few, has now become a way of life for many. While the cost of living is indeed increasing, squeezing the middle class, we are still far better off than the generations As global economies grow and air travel decreases in cost, travelling long distances is no longer just a dream, even if you don't have much disposable income. This democratization of travel has given rise to diverse trends.

And then, of course, there is the rise of China and its global dominance. According to the International Air Transport Association, China has risen to prominence in the aviation industry, contributing to much of its growth. In 2022 China's GDP increased by 3 percent while the US grew just 2.1, according to Statistica. While a percentage may not seem like much, it represents the gradual shift of power. China, like it or not, is coming for the States, and it is expected to pass the States somewhere around 2040.

One of the most significant driving forces behind China's aviation growth has been the rise in domestic demand. An exploding middle class characterized by rising incomes has led to more Chinese citizens than ever before seeking the joys and conveniences of air travel. As the nation urbanized at an unprecedented pace, the demand for better connectivity between its cities became paramount. China is a big country—both when measured by population and space. Both short-haul flights connecting nearby cities and long-haul ones bridging the vast expanse of the country became staples, making China one of the most bustling aviation markets globally.

Keeping pace with this increased demand, China embarked on a vast and ambitious journey of infrastructure enhancement. The country now boasts a series of state-of-the-art airports, with Beijing Daxing International Airport being a testament to China's grand vision for the future of aviation. Concurrently, recognizing the need for highly skilled individuals, China established a variety of aviation training academies and schools to cultivate and nurture the next generation of aviation professionals.

While every country suffered under COVID, China was one of the countries that was hit hardest by the virus, and, most likely because of the strict government-mandated lockdowns, it has seen a slower recovery than North America's aviation industry. Thankfully, after China reopened its borders, both the national and international passenger influx has been showing signs of recovery.

If anything, COVID clearly demonstrated just how important aviation is not only in direct job creation but also all the jobs that are indirectly created by travel and tourism. And with the full recovery of China on track, China's aviation will be very interesting to watch over the next couple of decades.

At the core of aviation's economic imprint are the direct jobs which encompass roles within airlines, airports, and aircraft manufacturing companies. These jobs are the immediate cogs in the aviation machinery, ensuring seamless operations from take-off to touchdown. However, the economic benefit of aviation doesn't end here. There are also indirect jobs generated through the supply chain catering to the aviation industry. This encapsulates a variety of businesses, including hospitality, hotels, shops and the hundreds of other types of local businesses that benefit from tourism.

Let's start by diving a little deeper into the jobs that are directly tied to the aviation industry. And I can't think of a better place to begin than perhaps the sexiest of jobs first—the plane's pilots. These men and women are the rockstars of the skies. As the most recognized category, airline pilots are responsible for transporting millions of passengers across the globe. As pilots reach the mandated age of retirement of 65, new pilots and first officers (co-pilots) are always in demand, especially with the exponential growth of air travel, which is anticipated in the coming decades.

It's worth remembering that not all pilots fly people. Some are responsible for ensuring goods reach their destination on time. While the shipments of goods are far more cost-effective and a much more common way of getting goods across the world, we should not discount the increasing demand for air transport—especially as online shoppers expect their packages to arrive inimitably on their front door.

Of course, air travel would not be nearly as comfortable without flight attendants. While we won't cover flight attendants, customer service positions, and other entry level jobs as much in this book, that doesn't make them any less important to the flight experience. I have worked as a flight attendant several times in my life, and believe you me, air travel wouldn't be possible without them.

It's a common misconception that flight attendants primarily serve food and drinks, but the in-flight crew's actual job is the safety of those on board. Flight attendants face a rigorous screening process. They must be trained on every emergency possible or in the event of a medical emergency. With their training and inherent people skills, they must diffuse tension, offer solutions and ensure that every passenger feels heard and cared for—not an easy job by any means!

We will next move on to the air traffic controllers (or ATCs). This is one of the most challenging careers in aviation, but a rewarding one. It's not an easy feat managing the take-offs, landings and ground control traffic. Managing all this, especially at a busy airport during peak travel times, is stress-inducing, to say the least! Yet these professionals maintain calm and make split-second decisions that affect hundreds of lives. Their role is often cited as one of the most challenging in the world—both mentally and emotionally, and so it takes a special type of person to enter into this type of job.

Next on the list is aircraft engineers. Every plane in the sky represents a culmination of research, engineering, manufacturing, and testing. Each component, be it a turbine or a tiny screw, is the resulting product of many diverse businesses all over there world.

It's important to note, the aviation industry is not merely a mode of passenger travel, but it is also used for the transportation of goods. While the amount of cargo transported by air is small compared to freighter and land – only 2 percent of the world's cargo – aviation accounts for 30 percent of the global value, a testament to its indispensable role in moving high-value commodities across borders.

Recently, aviation has also witnessed an uptick in commercial flights, aviation routes, and miles flown by aircraft, and flight hours. This burgeoning activity in the sky reflects a substantiating 65.5 million jobs and injecting a hefty 3.6 percent into the global GDP. This economic windfall is propelled by the diverse cargo that air transport ferries around the globe.

At the heart of air cargo's value proposition is its ability to swiftly and securely transport high-value items. This includes a cornucopia of goods such as cellphones, technology, high-end automobiles, and even rare and exotic animals. The urgency of air transport becomes even more palpable when it comes to shipping time-sensitive items like fresh produce, human organs for transplant, or even the solemn task of transporting the deceased. Moreover, the skies also serve as a conduit for moving significant volumes of cash, gold, and gemstones, underlining the secure and expeditious nature of air transport.

The horizon looks promising for the aviation sector with future projections indicating a steady climb. An average growth rate of 4.3 percent per annum over the next two decades underscores a trajectory of expanded economic interconnection. This growth is set to further augment employment opportunities, elevate the contribution to global GDP, and naturally, increase the number of daily flights crisscrossing the skies. Undoubtedly, as more goods take to the skies, the economic impact will resonate through the job market, GDP figures, and beyond.

Okay, so we've covered some of the jobs that are a direct result of the aviation industry and ways airplanes transport cargo, what about the indirect jobs and the indirect way aviation effects Global GDP? While it's easy to identify the direct jobs within the aviation sector, the indirect job creation is vast and equally essential, but harder to quantify. (Although the International Civic Aviation Organization does its best to estimating these numbers.) As most of us noticed during COVID, our cities are incredibly different when there are no tourists visiting, most of whom come by air.

Just looking at Vancouver, for example, the city I grew up in, a significant portion of revenue comes from tourism and hospitality—$14.4 billion and over 105,000 jobs. Granted, some of that revenue comes from cruise ships, but many come from air. And this is just one city and one example. In 2021, visitors spent $52 billion in the Big Apple. But what about the rest of the United States? Tourists spend around $190.40 billion a year in the United States. That's $190 billion! How much is from air travellers alone? It's impossible to say because there are no records that separate the data by modes of travel. I can only speculate: The States is a vast country and according to Airlines for America, the United States operates more than 25,000 flights, carrying more than 2.5 million passengers daily. So, it's safe to say, that the impact of the aviation industry on the economy is monumental.

Chapter 2:
Aviation By Region

While we've talked about aviation as a whole, it obviously differs from region to region. Each continent, with its own geography, culture, and economic situation, has a unique aviation ecosystem that reflects its own distinct identity. For example, in continents like Asia, Africa, and North America, much of the population is spread out over a wide distance, making air travel more of a necessity for those wishing to travel over those distances. This is not the case in Europe, which has a long history of transportation, and its dense population is more connected by (often cheaper) high-speed trains, which forces air travel to be more competitive.

However, perhaps, the most important factor is the economics of a nation, which can dictate how often people travel by air. For example, while Africa is a vast continent, home to 1.2 billion people, 13 percent of the world's population, Africans still travel very little by air compared to other regions. This is in stark contrast to the United States, one of the richest countries in the world, which operates 25,000 flights carrying 2.5 million passengers daily. That's daily! Not only that, the U.S. accounts for 62.5 percent of all the world's private jets, according to Airbus.

Another interesting note about the aviation industry is that, much like the internet, it doesn't work without global cooperation and coordination. This is why the founders and early entrepreneurs who championed aviation recognized that no country should be left behind. Therefore, in this spirit, resources are made available globally for training and development.

In this chapter, we'll look at each region separately to see how it has developed and what its current role is in aviation.

North America

Let's start with North America, which has the most mature aviation industry. North America, with a population density of 20 individuals per square kilometer, is home to nearly 579 million people, accounting for 4.7 percent of the global populace. This region, according to 2023 statistics from Worldometer, is witnessing an urban boom, with 83 percent of its residents dwelling in cities.

The impact of this urbanization is, of course, profoundly felt in the aviation sector. Airports have become pivotal economic engines, and their success hinges on proximity to these large urban populations. A 2023 Statista report underscores the importance of such urban hubs to the region's Gross Domestic Product (GDP).

North America is home to some of the biggest airlines when it comes to revenue, planes, and employees: Delta, American Airlines, and United are powerhouses within the industry. Airline performance is often measured by Revenue Passenger Kilometers (R.P.K.), and in this metric, United Airlines leads with the highest R.P.K. of 29.3 billion, capturing 4.9 percent of the global market share. American Airlines and Delta also show strong performances, indicating the competitive and healthy state of American carriers.

When it comes to air travel, North America's airports lead the world in terms of passenger volume. Data from the International Civil Aviation Organization (ICAO) in 2018 highlighted that the busiest airports for departures in North America were Chicago, Atlanta, Los Angeles, and Dallas. These figures reflect the robustness of the aviation industry in these cities and, by extension, across the continent. Atlanta Airport, in particular, has set records with an annual passenger volume exceeding 4.45 million, followed closely by Los Angeles with over 3.47 million passengers. This significant flow of people through these airports showcases the vibrant nature of air travel in North America.

In the realm of cargo, Memphis stands out as the second busiest for freight transport, closely following Anchorage, Alaska. Why Alaska? Anchorage's strategic Arctic location makes it a pivotal freight transfer hub, linking Asia and North America and underscoring the global reach of the region's aviation industry.

The economic backdrop of this thriving aviation scene is North America's substantial GDP, which stands at $31,319 billion, or 29.7 percent of the world's total, second only to Asia. The robust economy ensures that air transport services are widely available and integral to the region's infrastructure. The North American Free Trade Agreement (NAFTA), signed in 1994, has further bolstered economic activity, stimulating trade and travel between Canada, the U.S., and Mexico.

In terms of future prospects, North America has a staggering 3,528 aircraft on order, with the U.S. accounting for the majority, signalling ongoing growth and expansion in air travel capacity. The region also boasts a high number of registered aircraft, with the U.S. leading and Canada holding a strong position globally.

This high-level overview of North America's aviation landscape paints a picture of an area that is not just thriving but also strategically poised for future growth, with urbanization and economic strength driving the success of its airline industry.

However, perhaps, the biggest part of what makes the North American aviation industry so prominent is that it is home to some of the biggest airplane manufacturers, including Boeing, Lockheed Martin, and General Electric. It helps that many of America's top aviation companies are mainly fuelled by the United States' large defence budget.

As the largest builder of commercial airlines, Boeing has a huge impact on North America's aviation landscape, as well as across the globe. One of its prime contributions is, of course, economic. Boeing is a significant job creator, based on its website, it employs around 145,000 people in 65 different countries as well as sustaining a vast network of suppliers and partners. As one might expect, the ripple effect of its operations goes beyond the aviation sector, influencing broader industrial and economic landscapes.

In addition, the essence of innovation at Boeing has been a catalyst for advancements in aviation technology. With a legacy that spans over a century, Boeing has been at the forefront of many breakthroughs. From pioneering jet travel with the iconic 707 to revolutionizing long-haul flights with the 787 Dreamliner, Boeing's innovation has continually pushed the boundaries of what's possible in the skies. This relentless pursuit of innovation not only fosters a culture of excellence within North American aviation but also sets a global benchmark with companies like Airbus in its wake.

Furthermore, Boeing's commitment to sustainability is a testament to its foresight and responsibility. As the global aviation industry grapples with environmental challenges, Boeing's endeavors to reduce emissions and enhance fuel efficiency resonate as crucial steps towards a sustainable aviation future. The ecoDemonstrator program, for instance, is a good example of Boeing's drive to test and accelerate sustainable aviation technologies.

However, as one might suspect with any company that is a hundred years old, the journey has not always been smooth. Boeing has faced its share of challenges, like when two 737s crashed, killing over 346 passengers, grounding the plane. Yet, these adversities also reflect Boeing's capacity for learning, adapting, and maintaining a steadfast commitment to safety and quality.

Europe

Next, I want to move on to Europe. While the Wright brothers are generally credited with flying the first airplane, a lot of interesting experimentation and advancement were done in Europe. For example, in 1905, Gabriel and Charles Voisin founded the world's first commercial airplane factory in France.

The first officially recognized flight in Great Britain was in 1908 when showman Samuel Franklin Cody partnered with the British army to fly the British Army Aeroplane No 1. Cody continued to experiment and build airplanes, winning the Michelin Cup in 1910 for the longest flight made in England.

Europe does not like to be outdone by its North American counterparts and the same goes for aviation; Europe is a powerhouse rivalling any other continent. It accounts for 26.2 percent of overall aircraft traffic and serves over 1.1 billion passengers each year.

With 50 countries in Europe, the continent could not work as efficiently as it does without its open skies policy, which fosters an environment where airlines can navigate across borders with minimal regulatory hindrances. The benefits of the Open Skies Policy extend beyond the aviation industry, helping generate economic activity across Europe. It has made air travel more accessible, connected cities, fuelled tourism, and increased trade, thereby contributing significantly to the European economy. Moreover, the policy has accelerated the pace of innovation in the aviation sector, with airlines and airports continually embracing cutting-edge technologies to enhance operational efficiency, safety, and sustainability.

Germany is the economic powerhouse in Europe and its home to the Lufthansa Group, which is one of the biggest and most important airlines in the world. As of 2022, its fleet comprised over 700 aircraft, transporting more than 145 million passengers annually. Meanwhile, the Franco-Dutch merger between Air France and KLM has given rise to another European aviation powerhouse, Air France-KLM. With a history dating back to the early 20th century, these two airlines are among Europe's oldest. In 2021, Air France-KLM operated a fleet of approximately 550 aircraft, carrying around 87 million passengers, showcasing its vast operational scale and reinforcing its status as one of the most prestigious airline groups in the continent.

Turning to manufacturing, one of Europe's biggest players in building commercial planes is Airbus. Much like the Open Skies policy, Airbus is a testament to cross-country collaboration. Born from a consortium of aerospace manufacturers from France, Germany, Spain, the Netherlands and the U.K., Airbus is a symbol of what Europe can achieve when countries work together.

In the late 1960s, Europe's aviation industry was scattered, with various nations having their own individual aircraft manufacturers. Facing tough competition from American giants like Boeing, Lockheed, and McDonnell Douglas, European companies realized that joining forces was the only way to compete effectively on a global scale. The result was Airbus which was established in 1970.

The first aircraft to wear the Airbus badge was the A300, the world's first twin-engine widebody jet. Launched in 1972, the A300 showcased Europe's engineering prowess and commitment to challenging American companies. The A300's success laid the groundwork for Airbus's expansion into various segments of the commercial and military aviation market.

The A310, a derivative of the A300, followed shortly, featuring a shorter fuselage and new wings. This plane demonstrated Airbus's vision of commonality, where multiple aircraft types shared similar cockpits, systems, and handling characteristics, thus reducing training and maintenance costs for airlines.

Then, in the 1980s, Airbus unveiled the A320, a pioneering single-aisle aircraft. The A320 family, which expanded to include the A318, A319, A321, and the New Engine Option variants, became popular in the single-aisle market.

In 2007, after years of development, the A380 made its commercial debut. Recognized as the world's largest passenger airliner, the A380 can carry over 800 passengers in a typical two-class configuration. Large planes are thought to be typically American, but Airbus proved that they could challenge and even exceed their American counterparts with the double-decker giant, showcasing Airbus's ambition and engineering capabilities.

Furthermore, just like Boeing, Airbus's commitment to sustainability aligns with Europe's broader environmental objectives. Its ambition to lead in the decarbonization of the aviation sector resonates with the continent's green transition goals. Initiatives like the ZEROe program, which aims to develop the world's first zero-emission commercial aircraft, underscore Airbus's pioneering role in driving the industry towards a sustainable future.

On the global stage, Airbus's rivalry with Boeing has epitomized the dynamics of global aviation competition. By holding its ground and often outpacing its rival in key aspects, Airbus has showcased the prowess and potential of European aviation on a global canvas.

Today, the economic effect of Airbus is felt far beyond just Europe; the company has recently expanded operations into Canada, China, and even the United States, as well as other emerging markets.

Africa

Africa presents a unique opportunity in the global aviation arena. Unfortunately, the journey towards realizing Africa's full potential is often beset with roadblocks, prominently underdeveloped infrastructure, government delay, and underfunded airlines. These hurdles not only stall the growth of the African aviation industry, but also thwart the continent's ability to magnetize high volumes of passengers, thus leaving much of the potential unexplored. The lack of substantial investment translates to outdated fleets, limited network expansion, and a struggle to meet international operational standards. This financial crunch is a significant barrier, keeping many airlines from their full potential.

Amidst its many challenges, the continent's aviation sector displays glimmers of promise, largely embodied by success stories like that of Ethiopian Airlines. With its expansive network and commendable operational efficiency, the airline epitomizes what African aviation can achieve with the right mix of investment, governance, and strategy. It's a testament to the possibilities that lie within the continent, waiting to be harnessed.

There are also other reasons to be optimistic. The increased demand for connectivity, driven by a growing economy and a youthful population, holds promise for aviation growth. Moreover, initiatives like the Single African Air Transport Market (SAATM) is an example of government policy done right; much like what Europe has done with its Open Skies Policy, SAATM is a significant move towards creating a more integrated and collaborative aviation ecosystem across the continent and it is a cornerstone initiative of the African Union Agenda 2063. Designed to unify Africa's air transport sector, it will help increase economic cooperation, trade, employment and tourism, benefiting all of Africa in numerous ways that stretch far beyond aviation. IATA is a huge supporter of the SAATM initiative, seeing it as a pathway to unlock the full potential of African aviation. An IATA study indicates that if 12 major African nations liberalized their air markets, it could result in an additional 155,000 jobs and augment the GDP by US$1.3 billion annually in those nations. As of now, the SAATM initiative has garnered the commitment of 34 countries.

The Middle East

The Middle East aviation market is extremely unique. Its size is estimated to be at $62.50 billion and it is expected to reach $72 billion by 2028, growing at a rate of 2.89 percent during the foreseeable future. It's also predicted that the Middle East's share of the global fleet will grow from 4.9 percent in 2023 to 6 percent in 2033, while the global fleet is projected to expand by one-third to over 36,000 aircraft by 2032.

Prominent carriers like Emirates, Etihad, and Qatar Airways, while they may not have as storied history as their American or European counterparts, are set to be extremely competitive for long-haul routes, especially in significant hubs like Dubai, Istanbul, and Doha, which are ranked among the world's busiest airports. In addition, new airlines are emerging, like Saudi Arabia's RIA airlines, augmenting the competition and offerings in the Middle East.

However, perhaps the most significant factor in the Middle East's aviation market, especially in recent years, is the benefits from state-led initiatives to boost tourism and business travel, such as mega-events like the Dubai Expo, and World Cup in Qatar, which significantly contribute to passenger traffic and, in many ways, puts the Middle East on the map. The region is also investing in technology and sustainability initiatives to ensure its aviation sector aligns with global trends toward digitization and reduced carbon emissions.

South America

The South American aviation sector is an interesting market that presents a mix of notable strengths and significant obstacles. One of the most important factors contributing to South America's aviation is the region's abundant and unique tourist destinations that attract global visitors—

Machu Picchu, the Iguazu Falls, the Galapagos, and the Amazon Rainforest are just a few examples.

In addition, the continent's strategic positioning and increasing global economic dominance is important for connecting flights across the Americas, Europe, and other parts of the world, with major hubs like São Paulo, Bogotá, and Santiago being essential for these international routes. In addition, a testament to the region's strength is Mercosur, the prominent free trade agreement between Argentina, Brazil, Paraguay, Uruguay, and Venezuela. This economic powerhouse exemplifies the success that can be achieved when neighboring countries with shared cultural and linguistic ties come together to foster economic integration.

One of the key factors that simplifies aviation in Latin America is the predominance of Spanish and Portuguese. This linguistic homogeneity, as opposed to the 24 different languages spoken in Europe, ensures clearer communication and understanding among different airports and airlines.

However, the industry faces considerable challenges. Airports across South America, like many across the world, often struggle with outdated facilities and congestion, affecting flight efficiency and passenger convenience. But perhaps the most significant factor is the economic and government landscape is unpredictable, with currency fluctuations and political upheaval sometimes hindering the aviation sector's expansion and fiscal health.

In addition, despite having a wealth of oil and gas in the region, airlines grapple with high operating expenses, mainly costly aviation fuel and various taxes, which can lead to increased ticket prices. Intense competition following deregulation puts financial strain on airlines, sometimes resulting in market consolidation or the folding of airlines. The regulatory environment, despite efforts toward deregulation, is still fraught with bureaucratic barriers and lacks uniformity, making operations complex for carriers active in multiple South American countries.

Lastly, ongoing corruption deters investment, inflates costs, and increases danger, all of which have consequences within the aviation sector and its employees. For Latin America to fully capitalize on its tourism and aviation potential, a concerted effort to combat corruption is essential. Strengthening governance, enhancing transparency, and enforcing stringent anti-corruption measures can help the region reach a higher altitude in global competitiveness, ensuring that its skies and tourism prospects remain clear and promising.

Asia

Lastly, we have perhaps the most interesting region: China, which is at the forefront of Asian aviation. Ever since the 1980s, the Chinese economy has really started to take off, and combined with the increased aspirations of its growing middle class – who wish to travel more and further – it comes as no surprise that China's aviation industry has steadily grown.

China and India, in particular, represented major growth areas within Asia's aviation sector, with forecasts suggesting they would become the world's first and third-largest aviation markets by the 2030s, respectively.

As the world watches, carriers like Emirates, Cathay Pacific, and Singapore Airlines are capitalizing on the surging demand, turning cities like Dubai, Shanghai, and Beijing into bustling global aviation hubs. However, amidst the upward trajectory, challenges like infrastructure lag and airport congestion have caused problems. Yet the future is promising, with a projected annual growth of 5.6 percent in passenger trips over the next two decades.

But many low-cost airlines, AirAsia and IndiGo are just two examples, which are vying for tourism dollars, and have aggressively expanded their market share by offering significantly lower ticket prices compared to full-service carriers. This is often achieved through operational efficiencies such as using a single aircraft type to reduce maintenance costs, employing dynamic pricing strategies, operating from secondary, less-expensive airports, and maximizing aircraft utilization with quick turnaround times between flights.

Last Thoughts

Unsurprisingly, aviation across the globe is not homogeneous. Each region has its own strengths and its own challenges that it must overcome. While mature markets like North America and Europe have traditionally dominated the aviation industry in terms of technological advancements, high-caliber companies, and economic achievements, that does not necessarily mean they won't be overtaken by other regions such as China or even the Middle East in the next couple of decades.

While the growth path of aviation is clear: what it will look like in the future is anybody's guess. What is known is that the same spirit of collaboration, adventure, and competition will continue to foster in the new age. And it is the younger generation who will bring these ideals into aviation to solve the bigger problems the industry faces.

Chapter 3:
The World Of Airports

At the heart of air travel, we have airports. Now, we've all travelled through them to our destinations. For most people, airports are a transfer point—a necessary evil to get to where we want to go. Often, we remember hustling through the terminal, listening to the announcements over the loudspeaker about how it's the last call to board your plane, or being lost in some foreign airport, trying to find the place we need to be. All in all, airports have many challenges, but it's often undeserved considering all the working parts that go into making an airport run smoothly.

Airports are fascinating places. They are also the first impression of a different country and sometimes even a different culture. And the best airports understand this. You step onto the conveyor belts in Dubai, and you pass through a row of beautiful palm trees, or visit the rooftop pool in Singapore's airport, or the largest terminal in the world, a breathtaking display of architecture, inspired by the shape of a starfish in Beijing, and you understand you are in for an entirely new experience.

The Airport Master Plan

Not many people know that airports have Master Plans, which are long-term visions for the airport, often spanning 20 years. These plans look at the airport from every aspect: from how they can improve passenger congestion, use the airport's land, runway capacity and possibly runway extension, airport upkeep and expansion, and how to minimize environmental impact are just a few key areas of focus.

The implementation strategy of the Master Plan involves deciding on which projects to move forward with based on priority, feasibility, and financial viability. The Master Plan is also a guide to actively involve stakeholders such as airlines, retailers, environmental organizations, the community and governmental organizations in the planning process to address concerns and gather insights into how to tackle the larger problems that face airports. In some ways, reading an airport's Master Plan is like looking into a crystal ball, predicting where many of the job opportunities will be.

While reading a Master Plan might not be a Stephen King novel, it's worth taking a look at several Master Plans from different airports as they can help you understand the challenges that airports face and how they plan to overcome them. A quick Google search will help you find several Airport Master Plans. Reading these documents is especially important for people who want a career in aviation because it helps them understand how airports think about the future.

Also, it's important to note when an airport is using its resources to overcome these challenges, that means they are employing people. You might be surprised at the different types of jobs that are available—some which you might not have considered as careers so it's worth taking a look, and seeing what is out there.

The Cost of Congestion

A bad experience at an airport can sour an entire trip. You lose your luggage, miss a connecting flight, or have problems at security, and you already feel a little stressed and angry starting a vacation. While these may seem like minor annoyances that are just a necessary evil when taking an airplane, if you take a step back and look at the macro level, you'll find people make important travel decisions based on how convenient it is to travel to a place, which can impact the economics of a city and even an entire country.

Although somewhat inefficient, it probably doesn't seem like a big deal. Yes, it probably is only a minor inconvenience, but when you add up all the small delays like that, you can get a very frustrating travelling experience. And then you multiply the thousands of people who go through Addis Ababa, and it really takes an economic toll on the airport. It's just human nature to like convenience. Nobody likes to wait around which is why it's important to be able to process people efficiently while still ensuring all the security and checkpoints are in place.

Unsurprisingly, people take the path of least resistance when they travel. Would I have gone to Ethiopia if I had not been selected to speak at a TED Talk? As beautiful of a country as Ethiopia is, it's a long way from my native Toronto, and not to mention expensive, and so it would not have been my first choice as a vacation getaway. I would much rather go to somewhere that is easier to get to. Will I pass through Paris if I can avoid it? Absolutely! Now, of course, not all of that is in the hands of the airports. Some of it's just by chance.

Atlanta is one of the busiest airports not because everybody is rushing to go to Atlanta, but because it's fairly centralized to many other destinations and has a 5 parallel runway design which allows it to process the number of planes and passengers it does; people would find different routes. According to the Economist, The European Organisation for the Safety of Air Navigation, commonly known as Eurocontrol, estimates the cost of air traffic management delays in Europe alone to be €17.6 billion. In other words, people vote with their feet. There is only so many delays and poor customer service people will tolerate. If an airport can't handle the traffic, people will travel elsewhere.

Delays Aren't Just Annoying

When we look up at the big electronic board in the middle of the airport, and we see that our flight has been delayed, our first thought is about the inconvenience—which is understandable, but I want to look at the economic impact these delays have on the economy. It's a cascading effect that leads to unforeseen expenses, both for the passengers and for airlines.

While many travel destinations have a non-refundable policy, travel hiccups mean less time and money is spent at certain restaurants, in museums, or tourist hotspots. Airport hotels, restaurants, coffee shops, and souvenir stores benefit from delays, while airlines are often get the brunt of the anger from passengers who blame the airlines, even when it's not their fault. This can lead to people booking alternative airlines if they have had a bad experience.

In the past, experts have not considered the mental health component of both passengers and staff alike. Thankfully, in recent decades, mental health has been a real focus, and it is less stigmatized to talk about it. Frayed nerves, the stress of having to change plans and dealing with frustrated family members can take a real toll. While this story might be anecdotal, I heard of two sisters who went to Australia. One sister did all the planning, the other did not. When they reached their destination, the one sister who had planned the entire trip was so frustrated that her sister didn't even thank her, she turned around and booked a trip back home, leaving the other sister to travel by herself. While vacation is supposed to be enjoyable and relaxing, sometimes it's quite the opposite.

Then there is also the mental health of the airport staff to consider, who have to deal with stressed-out travellers day in and day out who can sometimes be rude and abusive. Just as doctors and nurses are at the brunt of the healthcare worker shortage, so too, airport workers have to deal with a system that is bending, if not breaking. In a survey by the IATA, airport staff cited congestion as a top stressor, with impacts on both emotional and physical health through increased risk of communicable diseases in cramped spaces.

Then there is the wear and tear to the airports themselves. Like many of North America's infrastructure, airports were built after the post-war boom and although have had upgrades since then, they are slowly beginning to show their age, especially facilities like JFK in New York and LAX in Los Angeles, the constant use of the runways and terminals have caused deterioration and frequent repairs, and service disruptions which add to the operating cost.

What Can Airports Do?

So far, it's only been doom and gloom. And yes, there are challenges, but there are also solutions. One of the biggest problems airports face is congestion and delays. The simplest answer to this is to use technology to increase the processing time. Perhaps one of the most transformative types of technology in airports is the use of real-time data analytics. By analyzing data from various sources such as flight schedules, passenger flow, and staff allocations, airports can make informed decisions to optimize operations across the entire airport.

Real-time data analytics helps in anticipating and managing disruptions, ensuring efficient resource allocation, and improving the overall passenger experience. For example, if a flight is delayed, real-time data can help airport staff to quickly rearrange gate assignments, notify passengers, and manage crowd control.

Real-time analytics can also efficiently manage ground vehicles, such as baggage carts, fuel trucks, and passenger shuttles, which play a vital role in reducing tarmac congestion and ensuring that planes can take off and land efficiently.

Airports are now employing sophisticated ground traffic management systems that use GPS and IoT (Internet of Things) technologies. These systems provide real-time tracking of vehicles, enabling better coordination and faster response times. For example, by knowing the exact location of baggage carts, airport staff can ensure quicker and more efficient baggage handling. (Anybody who wants to go into aviation management will have to understand how this software works, be able to look at the data, and be able to interpret the results.)

Today, self-service kiosks have become a staple at many airports, allowing passengers to check in and print boarding passes with just a few clicks. This shift not only speeds up the process but also offers travellers more control over their journey.

Similarly, automated baggage drop-off points are revolutionizing how luggage is handled. These systems allow passengers to tag and drop off their bags without assistance, significantly reducing wait times. By streamlining the check-in and baggage handling process, airports can handle a higher volume of passengers more efficiently, leading to reduced congestion and a better travel experience.

Lastly, biometric screening represents a significant leap forward in airport security and efficiency. Using technologies like facial recognition, fingerprints, or iris scans for identity verification, airports can greatly streamline the security checks and boarding processes. At Toronto

Pearson Airport, pilot projects testing biometric scanning, which give travellers access to café lounges have been rolled out. Once the testing phase has been completed and is successful, this technology will then be allied to other areas that have a larger impact.

This technology not only enhances security by reducing the chances of identity fraud but also offers a faster, more seamless experience for passengers. For instance, some airports have implemented biometric gates that scan passengers' faces as they board, eliminating the need to present boarding passes and identification documents repeatedly.

The Increasing Importance of Smaller Airport Hubs

According to Business Today, only about 4 percent of India's 1.4 billion people use planes as a mode of transportation, but that's looking to increase over the next 10 years. We'll likely see a massive influx of people use air transportation. At the moment, most airliners rely on large airports in places like London, Atlanta, Dallas and Paris to connect to places elsewhere in the world. However, these large airports are at critical mass and are at capacity of what they can handle both in terms of plane traffic taking off and landing, and processing passengers in the terminal.

However, there are medium-sized airports that could be ready to handle the increased volume. But these airports, if they don't approach the problem correctly, will have the same issues as the larger airports. After all, if the aviation industry just avoids the root problem, instead of trying to solve it, nothing gets better. It's akin to solving city congestion by doubling the size of the highway. That may seem like a good solution but what happens when double the traffic gets into the city roads which weren't designed for that many cars.

So, what's the answer? Physical expansion is the most visible response—a tangible sign of growth. Yet, this is not merely about adding more gates or extending runways; it's a comprehensive transformation that encompasses updating terminals, using more automation, and even AI or machine learning to make passengers' experience smoother, quicker, and more efficient. This encompasses everything from improving baggage handling systems, security screening protocols, and passenger onboarding, to ground service operations, learning from the mistakes of their bigger airports.

While computers and systemizing are important, there will also be an increased demand for baggage handlers, maintenance crews, security officers, and air traffic controllers. The issue lies in that different governing bodies are responsible for the different positions, and in some regards, they must work together to ensure a seamless experience for passengers.

This requires innovation, policy reform and, above all, money, which is in short supply, especially as there are other pressing issues that politicians and government organizations must contend with.

One of the advantages the smaller airports have over the larger airports is they are able to look to the Heathrows and the LAXs and see what they have done wrong and how they can avoid these mistakes. Large airports are often criticized for their congestion and delays, that are often the result of technical difficulties, labor disputes and just the sheer volume of passenger traffic. For example, Toronto Pearson was designed to handle around 25 million passengers per year, but now roughly twice that many people pass through its gates. These situations are compounded by the constant upgrades and construction projects, which, although are probably unavoidable, contribute to short-term delays.

With some planning and foresight, the smaller hubs can carefully plan the layouts of the airports, hire the right staff, and plan their expansion before it becomes critical. One important lesson is to develop contingency plans for when there are factors that disrupt operations such as technical failures, power outages, weather conditions or other emergencies.

Environmental Concerns of Airports

While airports grow and take on more passengers, one of the most pressing aspects is the environmental impact of airports. As airports grow larger and are in higher demand, they will have to figure out a way to balance environmental concerns with revenue-generating activities—not an easy thing to do. This includes efforts to use energy efficiently, manage waste sustainably, and reduce noise pollution. Making older airports more environmentally friendly is a considerable undertaking, often involving large-scale infrastructure changes—not something easily done, even if there is money in the budget to do so. It might involve shutting down entire terminals to be rebuilt from the ground up which could possibly take a year or more. The airport would be forced to turn away travellers who would have to make alternative arrangements. And once the terminal is rebuilt, there is no guarantee that the travellers (or airliners) would return, perhaps finding the alternative routes to be satisfactory.

Reducing the environmental impact of an airport is one of the toughest challenges stakeholders face. So how can they tackle this pressing issue? One of the most straightforward ways is by finding cleaner energy sources.

The first thing is to recognize that no two airports are alike in their energy consumption. Airports in colder climates like Toronto's Pearson Airport, use more energy than, say, Los Angeles' LAX, which is in a warmer climate. In the winter, Pearson's has to heat the terminals, keep engines running, de-ice runways and airplanes before they take off, which takes additional energy and resources. While LAX will use air conditioning to cool their terminals, they will use less energy in their daily operations.

While it might be possible to find ways to increase efficiency and therefore, reduce the energy needed, it's easier just to switch to cleaner energy like solar or wind power. Of course, this might not work for all airports, again depending on where the airport is situated, but cleaner energy is definitely a step forward.

For example, Cochin International Airport in India has pioneered a private-public partnership that is a groundbreaking model that has made great strides in renewable energy. This large project features over 46,000 solar panels spread across 45 acres, generating 50,000 to 60,000 units of electricity. Over the next 25 years, this green power project is projected to replace over 300,000 tons of carbon emissions, akin to planting millions of trees or taking countless cars off the road. This project has achieved 'power neutrality," meaning its completely self-sustaining, making it the first airport to achieve such distinction.

In transforming itself into a solar powerhouse, Cochin International Airport has not only redefined its operational framework but also set a new benchmark for airports worldwide and what can be done with a little creativity, foresight, and willpower.

Another step is to use renewable energy like solar power or wind energy. A good example of this is Denver's airport. The airport recently built two new solar arrays, which boast a combined capacity of 18.5 megawatts. The arrays will generate an impressive 36 million kilowatt-hours of electricity annually. To put this into perspective, this amount of energy can power nearly 6,000 average homes in Denver every year.

Waste management represents a particularly thorny issue for the industry. The sheer volume of waste generated by airports and aircraft—ranging from disposable service items to decommissioned aircraft parts—is staggering. The solution lies in a multi-pronged approach that includes reducing the generation of waste, developing more sustainable materials, and implementing comprehensive recycling and upcycling programs. For instance, airlines can shift to using biodegradable or reusable service items. Airports can establish facilities for recycling and composting. Many airports, and indeed airlines have already made several strides forward in this regard.

Another renewable option is carbon emission offset. While this is better than nothing, it's far from ideal Carbon emission offsets function by enabling the purchase of credits that counterbalance one's emissions. This concept is rooted in funding projects like reforestation or renewable energy initiatives, which are designed to absorb or prevent an equivalent amount of greenhouse gases. The diversity of these projects allows for a wide range of actions, from planting trees to investing in clean energy technologies.

They provide a practical mechanism for reducing net emissions on a global scale. By financing green projects, offsets also create economic incentives for sustainable development. They offer flexibility for airports that might struggle with their own environmental initiatives.

But carbon offsetting has come under a lot of fire lately, primarily because it does not solve the larger environmental problems. In the past, companies use offsets more for public relations than for genuine environmental impact. The effectiveness of offsets relies heavily on stringent verification and transparency, which can be challenging to maintain. There's also a risk that focusing on offsets might delay more critical direct emission reduction efforts. Additionally, some offset projects can inadvertently lead to negative environmental or social impacts in the areas they are implemented, raising concerns about their overall sustainability.

The Role of Regulatory Bodies in Airports

While we may not see what goes on behind the scenes, regulatory bodies play a key part in airports. The foremost responsibility of regulatory bodies in airports is to maintain the safety and security of the passengers. These organizations establish comprehensive safety standards, conduct regular inspections, and audit airport operations to ensure compliance. They also oversee the implementation of stringent security measures to safeguard against threats such as terrorism and smuggling, ensuring a secure environment for passengers and staff.

To ensure that these standards are being met, regulatory bodies conduct regular inspections and audits of airport facilities and operations. These inspections can be scheduled or unannounced and cover various areas such as terminal safety, fuel storage, and emergency response capabilities. The findings from these inspections lead to improvements and, if necessary, enforcement actions to bring operations into compliance.

They also set rules for air traffic management, ensuring the safe and orderly flow of aircraft both in the air and on the ground. By regulating these operations, they help to minimize the risk of collisions and maintaining efficient flight schedules.

The Complex Synergy of Airplanes and Airports

Of course, airports and airlines need each other to operate, but that does not mean that they always have the same goals or objectives, and often it comes down to money. While airlines often chase the goal of quick turnaround times to keep their schedules on track, airports need to do more—and oftentimes, it's more advantageous for airports to keep travellers put. Why? Because for many airports, retail revenue is a significant income source. This means they can benefit from having passengers in their airports for extended times, encouraging travellers to spend more time in shops and restaurants. This fundamental difference in objectives can sometimes lead to tension, as what benefits one party may be detrimental to the other.

Airports and airliners have a concept that is known as the "golden hour." This critical window is the post-arrival and pre-departure time. For airlines, this period is crucial for efficient operations - refuelling, cleaning, and boarding need to happen swiftly. In contrast, airports view this hour as a golden opportunity for revenue generation, with passengers more likely to spend while waiting.

Understanding and acknowledging their distinct needs and constraints is the first step in harmonizing their movements. Only through collaboration and mutual understanding can the aviation industry soar to greater heights, providing efficient, enjoyable experiences for passengers and sustainable operations for both airlines and airports.

Challenges In Airport Layouts

The path forward for airport layout upgrades involves a holistic design approach that balances functionality, passenger experience, inclusivity, and sustainability. This process goes beyond architectural changes, delving into the social and environmental impact of these designs. Engaging with a diverse range of stakeholders and consultation with the public is vital in ensuring that the upgrades meet the needs of all its users.

As airports expand and become more intricate, the role of effective signage becomes ever more crucial. In North America, we like to think everybody speaks English, but that's not necessarily the case, so universally understandable signage is essential to guide passengers through the labyrinth of modern airport layouts. And it's not just a matter of slapping signage on where there is a spare. Upgrading signage should be systematic and requires a deep understanding of passenger flow and behavior.

Another significant challenge is ensuring bathrooms are inclusive and meet everybody's needs. Integrating gender-neutral bathrooms, family-friendly bathrooms, and wheelchair-accessible bathrooms is increasingly important. These facilities are essential for ensuring inclusivity and comfort for all travellers. However, retrofitting existing airports to include, for example, gender-neutral bathrooms can be a complex task, often requiring significant redesign and space reallocation. Again, this requires thought and planning.

Any future design must consider being fully accessible to people with mobility challenges. This includes wider aisles, accessible restroom facilities, ramps instead of stairs, and adequate space at check-in counters and security checkpoints. While many airports do a decent job of being wheelchair accessible, there is still a long way to go, even in the most advanced airports in the world. Recently a newspaper organization put a hidden camera on a person in a wheelchair who was flying from Toronto to Charlottetown. The hidden camera captured a multitude of issues, including staff struggling to transfer her between the aircraft and her wheelchair, equipment failure and, at one point, her ventilator was disconnected.

Lastly, creating different prayer rooms for the world's major religions helps promote inclusivity. These rooms need to be thoughtfully designed to cater to different religious needs. They should be easily accessible, well-signed, and located away from the bustling airport noise.

As more people use airports, it will be important to accommodate all types of people who have different abilities. In addition, with so much growth in countries like China and India, many of these people will be new to air travel, and so will need additional resources, be that signage or staff to answer questions. Airports will need to do a much better job. Airports will need to address these problems, evolve and embrace the challenges which comes with increased growth and demand.

The Funding of Airports

While most travellers are primarily concerned with getting from point 'A' to point 'B', rarely stopping to think about the economics of an airport, the financial models of how airports generate revenue are both fascinating and complex.

One of the primary sources of revenue is through airport fees, such as the use of runways, terminal facilities, and other aviation-related services. The charges are typically based on the weight of the aircraft and the number of passengers or the amount of cargo it carries. These fees are essential, as they directly relate to the primary function of an airport and keep everything operational.

However, there are secondary revenue streams which also add up, giving airports much-needed injection of money. Airports often host a variety of retail stores, from duty-free shops to luxury boutiques, alongside restaurants and cafes, contributing substantially to their revenue. Property leases present another lucrative avenue.

Airports lease space to airlines, retail shops, car rental companies, and other businesses. These leases are a steady source of income, providing financial stability and helping to diversify revenue streams. Advertising is yet another contributor. From billboards, signage, to digital displays, advertising spaces in airports are in high demand, and airport passengers are a captive audience.

Lastly, there are the parking fees which are a significant income source, especially at airports like LAX where public transport options are limited. There is generally short-term parking and long-term, with long-term parking trying to entice more frequent flyers with larger discounts and other perks. Some airports employ dynamic pricing strategies for their parking facilities. This approach allows them to adjust parking rates based on demand, time of the year, and even time of day. For example, parking rates can be higher during peak travel seasons or during special events. This pricing model helps maximize revenue from parking facilities. Then, of course, the airport can charge for shuttle services to the terminal, which provides additional revenue.

The future of airport revenue looks towards diversification and innovation. As air travel evolves, airports continuously adapt, seeking new ways to enhance passenger experience and generate income. The rise of digital technology offers opportunities for personalized retail and service experiences, potentially opening new revenue streams. Unfortunately, as airports age, and more upgrades are needed, more cash is needed to be interjected. These airports can't raise parking rates, they can't charge more at the duty free, or increase rents without a major outcry from the general public who already feel squeezed. So what can they do?

One effective way for airports to finance technology upgrades is through public-private partnerships. In these types of partnerships, an airport authority can collaborate with private sector companies to fund and manage specific projects. This partnership can take various forms, from private companies managing specific aspects of airport operations to complete private investment in airport infrastructure development. The success of public-private partnerships lies in leveraging the strengths of both sectors: the regulatory and public service experience of the government and the efficiency, innovation, and capital of the private sector. These partnerships can unlock private capital, reduce public expenditure, and bring in the expertise of private firms, making them a win-win for both parties. For instance, a tech company might finance the installation of advanced security systems in exchange for a long-term contract to manage those systems.

The Future of Airports

There are definitely challenges as the aviation industry grows. However, the skilled younger generation of workers, who are moving into management and leadership roles, will help solve the problems facing airports. As more people worldwide are living more comfortably, and demand for what was once considered first-world benefits increases, there will be a greater spotlight, which will ensure that the proper resources go into airports and their maintenance.

The biggest problem will undoubtedly be the environmental factor, but it's not exclusively something that airports are dealing with. Humanity as a whole grapples with this as more of the world's population is lifted out of poverty and, as a result, use up more resources. These are big problems, and they will need the right amount of technological advancement, funding, and ingenuity. However, I am confident they will be solved, and the aviation industry will do its part.

At the forefront are the regulatory bodies that are tasked with the job of drafting and enforcing the policies that drive the aviation industry forward. In the quest to navigate the future, collaboration is key. The industry must work closely together, not just within its own ranks but with technology providers, environmental organizations, and policymakers. These collaborations can pave the way for shared initiatives, such as global carbon offsetting schemes or joint investments in sustainable aviation fuels.

Moreover, the industry must be proactive and constantly engage with the public, cultivating a culture of transparency and accountability. By openly communicating its goals and progress towards sustainability, aviation can build trust and garner support for its initiatives—and they must start immediately.

The legacy of today's decisions will be felt for generations, and the industry's commitment to navigating a sustainable future will be the benchmark by which its stewardship of the skies is measured. The key to ensuring all this is to provide the next generation with the knowledge and skills to ensure that they can make a difference.

Chapter 4:
The Role Of Airlines

We cannot imagine a world without airline companies. After all, they are everybody's favorite whipping boys. But all joking aside, where would we be without the large carriers? They have revolutionized travel, and in doing so, they have become an integral part of global economics and cultural exchange throughout the world.

According to the United Nations, the aviation industry supports 66.5 million jobs worldwide and has a global economic impact of 2.7 trillion, underscoring its vital role—and as flight travel becomes more economical, sustainable, and convenient, these numbers will only rise in the near future.

The History of Airline Companies

There are, of course, many airline companies across the world with their own philosophies, approaches, and target markets. Each company does battle for market share and customer loyalty. Some of which, like Virgin and British Airways, are stories onto themselves, but we won't go into the salacious details—instead I will leave that to others. I want to look at the major trends of the industry, and to do that, we'll briefly look at the history of some of the major airlines in the world. It's worth noting a lot of the legacy airliners have a similar history; they are perhaps more intertwined than other industries because they are heavily impacted by the global economy, global trends, and technology.

Starting off with North America, which, in many respects, has the most mature market and hosts some of the world's largest and most influential airlines, such as Delta, American Airlines, and United. Let's look at the airlines that are sometimes called the 'Big Three'.

Airlines In America

Their story begins, like many other carriers in the early 20th century with the merger of dozens of smaller airlines. The most significant of these was the merger of Southern Air Transport, Robertson Aircraft Corporation, and Colonial Air Transport in 1929, forming what would eventually become American Airlines. The merger was a response to the economics of the time when many companies – not just airliners – struggled to stay out of bankruptcy. Through this merger, American was able to cut costs, streamline business operations, and survive the Great Depression.

American Airlines is important not only because it's a major player in today's aviation industry, but because it introduced many innovations in the industry, including the first electronic booking system in the 1950s and later a more advanced computerized reservation system, which revolutionized how airlines managed their operations and ticketing.

A pioneer in transcontinental and international travel, American Airlines launched its first coast-to-coast service with the DC-3 in 1937 and began international flights in 1945. Throughout its history, American Airlines has continued to expand through mergers and acquisitions, perhaps most notably the acquisition of TWA in 2001 and a significant merger with US Airways in 2013, solidifying its status as one of the world's largest airlines.

Next, we have Delta which officially opened its doors in 1929. Over the decades, Delta has continued to experience gradual growth, serving routes in the south-eastern United States and steadily expanding its network after World War II. Key mergers and acquisitions, including those with Western Airlines in 1987, Northwest Airlines in 2008, and a historic partnership with Virgin Atlantic, which has expanded Delta's global reach. Today, Delta is recognized as one of the world's largest global airlines, renowned for its customer service, operational reliability, and technological innovation, such as being the first U.S. airline to offer all in-flight entertainment for free.

Lastly, we have United Airlines. Its origins can be traced back to the establishment of Varney Air Lines by Walter Varney in Boise, Idaho, in 1926. By 1932, Varney had also set up Speed Lines, which would later become known as Continental Airlines, following a rebranding in 1934. Varney Air Lines was notable for operating the United States' first airmail flight under a private contract on April 6, 1926. The company would become part of a conglomerate created by William Boeing, known as United Aircraft and Transport Corporation, which integrated aircraft manufacturing with air transport.

Lufthansa

As influential as the United States has been in the airline industry, it's not the only player. Lufthansa, like its storied American counterparts has a long and important history. While the Lufthansa we know today was officially founded in 1953, its lineage traces came before the Second World War to the original Deutsche Luft Hansa AG created in 1926, making it one of the world's oldest airlines. With a fleet comprising mainly of Convair 340s and later the Lockheed Super Constellation, the airline embarked on a journey to re-establish Germany's presence in the commercial aviation space. Its initial routes focused on European destinations, but during the 1950s, it started to fly across the Atlantic.

Lufthansa has always put emphasis on technological advancement, and was among the first to introduce jet aircraft into commercial service with the Boeing 707 in 1960, and later, the Boeing 747 in 1970 — the iconic 'Jumbo Jet' that revolutionized long-haul travel.

The fall of the Berlin Wall and the subsequent German reunification in 1990 presented Lufthansa with both challenges and opportunities. The airline played a pivotal role in reconnecting East and West Germany and expanded its operations to cover the newly accessible regions.

Today, Lufthansa is one of the largest airliners in Europe and is one of the five founding members of Star Alliance which is the world's largest airline alliance, founded in 1997 in Frankfurt. Lufthansa has continued to innovate, particularly in the realm of sustainability, and it continues to modernize its fleet with more fuel-efficient aircraft, investing in sustainable aviation fuels, and implementing carbon offset programs.

Air Canada

Many people dismiss Air Canada as a small, insignificant regional player, but it's remarkable transformation, resilience, and adaptation should be a lesson to all airline companies across the world.

From its humble beginnings to its current status as the flag carrier and largest airline in Canada, the company has navigated through numerous challenges and opportunities to become a prominent figure in global aviation. Today, it punches above its weight in terms of customer service, routes, and profitability.

Air Canada was originally established as Trans-Canada Air Lines (TCA) in 1937, with the mission to provide Canadians with a coast-to-coast air service. Its humble maiden voyage was a mail and passenger service on a Lockheed L-10A, flying from Vancouver to Seattle. As TCA expanded its services across the nation, it played a critical role in connecting over Canada's vast landscape and fostering economic growth.

In the 1960s, TCA was rebranded as Air Canada. This change coincided with the adoption of a modern jet fleet, including the introduction of the McDonnell Douglas DC-8, which set the stage for a new era of jet-set travel.

Over the decades, Air Canada continued to diversify its services and expand its reach. It championed innovations in passenger comfort and in-flight services, becoming a trendsetter in the industry. The airline's route network grew exponentially, connecting Canadians to every corner of the globe and bringing the world closer to Canada.

Today, Air Canada is recognized for its extensive network, modern fleet, and commitment to customer service. With a fleet that boasts state-of-the-art aircraft like the Boeing 787 Dreamliner and Airbus A220, Air Canada is also at the forefront of environmental sustainability in aviation. The airline has implemented various strategies, such as investing in more fuel-efficient planes, exploring alternative fuels, and committing to carbon-neutral growth.

The Staffing of Airliners

Staffing an airline is a complex operation that requires meticulous planning and strategic foresight. It's like a careful game of Tetris where all the parts must fit exactly. If one pilot gets sick and cannot operate an aircraft, the flight is endangered of not making it to its destination. If the flight cannot make it to its destination, perhaps, its scheduled maintenance cannot happen–and so on. Thankfully, airliners build in contingency plans to ensure everything goes smoothly, and crews are doubled up in case of illness or unforeseen circumstances.

Ultimately, as air travel demand continues to grow post-COVID, understanding how to staff an airline efficiently becomes essential for maintaining smooth operations and ensuring growth.

And while we usually think about air travel for business and pleasure, the movements of goods are equally (if not more) important and should not be overlooked. There is a significant shift in consumer behavior, with a preference for online shopping and expedited delivery, which has revolutionized the supply chain. This evolution directly impacts air cargo and overnight freight operations, requiring airlines to adapt by employing more cargo pilots, logistics experts, and support personnel to meet the changing demands. But more about that later.

The type and number of aircraft in an airline's fleet naturally influence staffing requirements. Larger aircraft or those that demand more technical expertise necessitate additional or specialized crew members. And as airlines expand their fleets to accommodate growth or replace retiring aircraft, they must also scale their workforce accordingly. If an airliner can't staff a route properly, they will likely lose it to an airliner that can.

On average, it takes about 100 employees to operate a single aircraft, including several pilot crews and many support staff. Most of these are behind the scenes, unseen by air travellers, but that doesn't mean they are any less important.

To anticipate staffing needs, airlines conduct thorough age bell curve studies to determine the rate at which different positions in the airline company will retire, identifying how many new staff must be recruited and trained over the next 15 years. This is an important process to ensure an airline can indeed remain competitive, pay staff, and turn a profit for its stakeholders.

Perhaps the most pressing position is that of the pilot because they are one of the most highly skilled positions and because they are the hardest to replace. Becoming a pilot is a significant investment in time and money, with a rigorous pathway that includes extensive training and certification. Wealthier countries often have the advantage in attracting pilots, offering higher wages, comprehensive benefits, and a desirable work-life balance. However, increasingly, airliners such as Emirates and Qatar Airways and other, newer, well-funded airlines are offering higher salaries to recent aviation graduates, which is especially attractive to younger pilots who have debts and student loans to pay off. This was not the case 20 or 30 years ago when North American and European legacy airlines could pick the crème of the crop without worry about being poached.

The Importance of the Unions

The history of aviation unions traces back to the early 20th century, coinciding with the birth of commercial aviation. The pioneers of these unions were visionaries who understood the unique challenges of the industry. During a time of heavy industrialization and when union busting was a common practice, they saw the need for a unified voice to represent the interests of those who took to the skies.

In those early days, the focus was primarily on safety and basic labor rights. Pilots, mechanics, and other aviation workers banded together to advocate for safer working conditions, reasonable working hours, and fair compensation. These initial efforts laid the groundwork for a more structured union movement within the industry.

The pilots' union shapes the careers of the men and women in the aviation industry and, by extension, the airline industry itself. A robust union wields the power to negotiate for better wages and improved work conditions, key factors that can encourage pilots to remain with their current employers. In an industry where experience and continuity are invaluable, the ability of unions to retain skilled professionals is a vital component of a stable and prosperous airline operation.

The Air Line Pilots Association (ALPA) is the largest pilot union in the world, representing 75,000 pilots across North America and wields significant power in the aviation industry. Its role is to lobby for the rights of pilots. For example, in 1994, an airplane crashed, killing 132; the National Transportation Safety Board ruled that pilot error was the cause, however the ALPA fought the decision and in the end, it was found the malfunction was, in fact, the rudder control of the B-737. This example showcases how a union is more than just negotiating salaries but can actually change how an airliner operates.

The importance of unions in the aviation sector cannot be overstated. They are more than just entities fighting for labor rights; they are the guardians of safety, quality, and fairness in the industry. Ultimately, unions ensure that the advancements in aviation don't overshadow the human element - the well-being and rights of those who work tirelessly to keep our skies safe.

The Aviation Regulatory Bodies

In conjunction with the unions, the regulatory bodies play an important influence on airline companies. Many of the organizations that oversee all aspects of aviation were first conceived and are based in North America. Without tight regulations and oversight, the aviation industry would be the wild, wild west of travel, with different rules applying to different companies, and would, in all truthfulness, be unworkable. Instead, the aviation industry has an impeccable safety record, and all the different companies and organizations that make up the aviation industry work relatively seamlessly together.

Regulations cover a variety of aspects, including passenger rights, baggage handling, and environmental considerations. Regular audits, inspections, and updates ensure that these rules evolve with technological advancements and lessons learned from past incidents. Adherence to these stringent standards is paramount, making air travel one of the safest modes of transportation in the world. Airports undergo a safety audit every two years, which is conducted by seven separate companies. As passenger volume increases, so must the safety and security of an airport, which may include adding additional fire safety, addressing wildlife in the area, or more detailed security checks. As airports grow globally, the next generation will find employment opportunities in all these roles as well.

Regulatory bodies, such as the International Civil Aviation Organization (ICAO), with its headquarters in Montreal, set international standards, while national civil aviation authorities, like the Federal Aviation Administration (FAA). implement and oversee standards within the United States.

Breakthroughs That Have Transformed Airlines

The airline industry has undergone significant changes, including many technological and operational advancements that have changed how airlines operate, making air travel safer, more efficient, and accessible to the middle class. There are, of course, so many, and we won't be able to cover them all in this chapter, but these are some of the major ones that have changed air travel.

One of the larger changes was, unsurprisingly, the development of the jet engine. Introduced in the late 1940s, during the end of World War II, jet engines replaced propeller-driven aircraft. This meant airliners could fly higher, faster, and over longer distances without the need to stop for refuelling. This innovation opened up new routes, making transatlantic flights easier and expanding international travel and global reach.

Another significant advancement was the introduction of wide-body aircraft like the revolutionary Boeing 747 in the late 1960s. These aircraft could carry significantly more passengers and cargo than their predecessors, leading to economies of scale that made air travel more affordable. Like so many other aviation advancements, the wide-body was first pioneered by the United States military as a means to better transport troops. While many modern airplanes like Airbus' A350 and A380 use the wide-body design, it is still the "Jumbo Jet" that remains one of the most widely recognised and iconic passenger airplanes to have ever existed. Ever since it first took flight, it has become a symbol of the democratization of air travel, enabling airlines to transport more people across the world than ever before.

The computer revolution has also helped to modernize the aviation industry and was another critical step forward. One example was a computerized reservation system, which allowed airlines to manage bookings more efficiently while reducing operational costs and minimizing overbooking issues. This allowed airliners and airports to process more passengers more efficiently on a daily basis.

Another important technology, again pioneered by the military, is called fly-by-wire, which was a substantial advancement in aircraft control systems. This replaced manual flight controls with an electronic interface, allowing for a smoother, more precise flight experience while reducing a pilot's workload.

And lastly, around the same time, the advancement of Air Traffic Control has been a vital contribution, making it easier to communicate with aircraft which helps to avoid collisions. The most notable is the NEXT Gen—a satellite-based global aircraft navigation system—alongside collaborative strategies such as airline code-sharing, are expected to boost air travel demand further. These advancements not only enhance operational efficiency but also require a workforce that is adept at managing and maintaining complex, modern systems.

The Rise of Low-Cost Airlines

Perhaps nothing has revolutionized the airline industry in recent times as the low-cost carriers also known as LCCs, reshaping not only airline business models but also consumer expectations and travel habits. These carriers identified and exploited a niche market by offering no-frills service and significantly lower fares than traditional airlines.

The pioneering success of Southwest Airlines, founded in 1971, and Ryanair, established in 1984, showed the industry there was a demand for this type of service and helped accelerate the shift from flight being just a business class venture to a travel option the middle class could afford. By drastically lowering the cost of travel, LCCs made flying accessible to a vast, untapped customer base. This democratization of air travel spurred a substantial increase in passenger volumes and inspired a new era of budget-conscious travel.

The LCCs' strategy is underpinned by a relentless focus on cost reduction. This included simplified fare structures, single aircraft type fleets to minimize maintenance and training costs, quick aircraft turnaround times, and the use of secondary airports with lower landing fees. They also streamlined operations by eliminating unnecessary services, such as free meals and assigned seating.

The success of LCCs was noted by legacy carriers and forced them to rethink their business strategies. Many established airlines responded by introducing their own low-cost subsidiaries or by adopting similar cost-cutting measures. They also began to offer more unbundling of products and offerings. This allows passengers to choose and pay for only the services they value—such as extra baggage, more leg room, sitting with your travel partner, and so on. Additionally, traditional carriers invested in improving efficiency and productivity, leveraging technology for better yield management and customer service so they could continue to be competitive.

The LCC model has proven to be sustainable and profitable, leading to its adoption in markets around the world especially in recent years, in China and India. LCCs have grown to dominate short-haul routes and have even begun to challenge traditional carriers on long-haul segments. Their growth has continued to apply downward pressure on fares, further stimulating market growth and making air travel more affordable.

How Airlines Are Catering to Their Elite Travelers

While LCC have redefined the industry, legacy carriers such as American, United and British Airways have found themselves in a vicarious position: they wish to attract the deal hunters, but they also realize that much of their revenue comes from business travellers who want the extra perks, including more personalized services, and more convenient boarding and offloading. They seek a seamless travel experience that minimizes stress and maximizes productivity. Although there are fewer business people than deal hunters, they do fly more often, and so airliners have to decide which type of flyer they want to cater to.

In the past, airliners have solved this problem by creating subsidies that market towards low-cost travellers while keeping their legacy brand geared towards business travellers. For example, Air Canada created Air Canada Tango, a low-cost flight option. These subsidies have had mixed results, with many of them going bankrupt or being rolled back into the legacy brands. However, despite the setbacks, they have proved to be an interesting opportunity for airliners to expand their customer base.

Enhancing the Airport Experience

To appeal to business class travellers, airlines must first understand their unique needs. The airport experience is often the first impression a business traveller has of an airline's service quality, setting the stage for the flight itself. Recognizing this, airlines are redefining their lounge offerings, transforming them into places of comfort and efficiency that cater to the needs and desires of the business class clientele.

Exclusive lounges have become more than just waiting areas; they are destinations in their own right, designed to provide a serene and luxurious environment. Here, travellers are given high-speed internet that is reliable and secure in case they want to send that last-minute email or attend a video conference without interruptions.

The addition of spa services is another luxury that sets these lounges apart. From back massages to facials, airlines are partnering with renowned wellness brands to offer treatments that rejuvenate and relax passengers before their flight, understanding that the well-being of travellers directly impacts their overall experience.

Even attention to detail is evident in the design elements as well in these lounges. Comfortable seating, ambient lighting, and noise-cancellation features all play a role in creating a calming atmosphere within a busy airport. Art installations and natural elements like indoor gardens or water features contribute to a sense of tranquillity or can be used as a point of reference for meeting points.

This thoughtful approach to the airport experience demonstrates how airlines are not just facilitating travel but are elevating it to an art form.

For travellers with means, this enhanced airport experience is not just a luxurious perk but a vital part of their journey that allows them to arrive at their destination refreshed, prepared, and ahead of the game. What's more, airlines are recognizing that business travel is not just for businesspeople, and that post-COVID people are more likely to blend business with personal. Therefore, premium lounges are starting to cater to the needs of children and young adults by installing play areas, video game centers, as well as menus that cater to a variety of appetites.

Elevating In-Flight Comfort

While many airplanes have prioritized squishing more seats into a smaller space, reducing leg and arm room, business travel offers the comfort and convenience for people who want to travel in style, and have the budget for in-flight perks.

Lie-flat seats have become popular additions to many first class cabins. These seats are pretty much what they sound like: they recline to a full 180 degrees, allowing passengers to rest in a completely horizontal position. Crafted with ergonomic design in mind, they offer a bed-like comfort that can be a game-changer for those looking to arrive well-rested. In some cases, privacy pods are provided, offering a secluded space for passengers to work, dine, or sleep without the intrusion of fellow travellers' glances or disturbances. Recently Air New Zealand launched a campaign around their skycouches.

The in-flight dining experience is another area where airlines can differ. Unlike the processed meals in LCC flights, meals in business class are crafted from high-quality ingredients and are presented more like a dining experience then a classical in-flight meal. Some carriers go even above and beyond that: their meals can reflect the route's origin or destination, offering a taste of place even while airborne.

In addition, flight attendants are trained to provide an attentive service, often anticipating the needs of business class travellers before they are expressed. This could mean anything from preparing a hot towelette while the passenger finishes a meal, to quietly refilling a glass of vintage red and white wine at the perfect moment.

The culmination of these efforts is an environment that not only elevates comfort but also enhances the overall well-being of business travellers. By prioritizing the finer details of the in-flight experience, airlines are ensuring that business class passengers stay happy and fly with them next time.

The Importance of Loyalty Programs

Another important feature of airlines are loyalty programs. Airlines have recognized that fostering loyalty is about more than just a transaction, it's about creating a relationship. As such, the loyalty program is a way to not only rewards travel but also enriches the entire customer journey.

Airlines are continuously enhancing their loyalty programs to offer a wider array of rewards. These programs go far beyond merely accumulating miles for flights. They have evolved into comprehensive offerings that include tiered status levels, each with its own set of unique benefits. As passengers ascend from one tier to the next, the perks become increasingly attractive, incentivizing continued patronage.

One standout service that epitomizes this new era of luxury travel is the provision of car shuttle services for business class passengers. This service, designed for those with connecting flights, adds an extra layer of convenience and luxury. Imagine disembarking from your flight and being greeted by a chauffeur-driven car waiting to whisk you to your next destination. This service eliminates the stress of navigating through a busy airport and ensures a smooth, comfortable transition between flights.

Air Canada, for example, offers a range of such premium services. Their Signature Service is not just about travel, it's about creating an exclusive experience. From expedited check-ins to access to exclusive lounges, the service ensures that every aspect of the journey is comfortable and hassle-free. Air Canada's dedication to premium service represents a broader trend among airlines to elevate the standard of business class travel.

Beyond the luxury and comfort, it's the personal touch that truly sets apart services like those offered by Air Canada. Their concierge service is a perfect example. This service goes the extra mile, attending to personal requests such as arranging flowers for a birthday celebration, handling dry cleaning, or even picking up bakery items. It's this attention to detail and personalized care that transforms a simple flight into a memorable experience.

Traditionally, business class was seen as the domain of the solo business traveller. However, this demographic is rapidly changing, with families increasingly opting for business class travel. Recognizing this shift, airlines are adapting their services. Air Canada's premium lounges, for instance, now include family-friendly amenities like kids' play areas, video games, and child-friendly menu options like hot dogs and macaroni. This shift not only makes business class more inclusive but also ensures that the needs of all passengers, regardless of age, are met with the same level of excellence.

Upgrades are among the most sought-after benefits, allowing travellers to experience the luxury of business or first-class without the additional expense. Complimentary lounge access is another key perk, providing a serene space to relax or work in before flights. Priority check-in, boarding, and baggage handling are also staple offerings that add convenience and efficiency to the travel experience.

Beyond the airport, partnerships with luxury hotels and car rental services extend the value of loyalty programs. Travellers can earn points or miles through stays at partner hotels or when renting vehicles, blurring the lines between aviation and broader travel experiences. These partnerships often include exclusive discounts, room upgrades, late checkouts, and other bespoke hotel services, enhancing the overall travel experience.

Credit card collaborations are another frontier airlines are exploring. Co-branded credit cards with Visa or Mastercard allow travellers to accrue points or miles on everyday purchases, accelerating the benefits earned. These cards often come with additional travel-related advantages such as travel insurance, no foreign transaction fees, and even annual travel credits, making them a powerful tool in a traveller's wallet.

Moreover, in an effort to outdo their competition, airliners are now partnering with a range of retail and lifestyle brands, enabling customers to earn miles through everyday shopping. This strategy not only drives customer engagement but also expands the airline's reach into new customer bases.

The ultimate goal of these loyalty programs and partnerships is to create a seamless ecosystem where every action a traveller takes can potentially enhance their flying experience. By providing a variety of ways to earn and redeem points, airlines are ensuring that loyalty programs remain relevant, valuable, and integrated into the lifestyles of their customers.

Chapter 5:
A Good Career Path?

The aviation industry, like many other high-skill fields, is currently facing a significant challenge: labor shortages. With an annual growth rate of approximately 4.3 percent, the aviation sector is projected to double in size every 16.74 years. This growth, while indicative of the sector's robustness, brings to light the urgent need for infrastructure development and skilled personnel.

This issue is becoming increasingly critical as the industry continues to grow at a substantial rate while the cost of schooling and the demands for jobs are increasing, which are contributing to fewer people choosing aviation as a career.

ICAO's Human Resource Development Study

The 2010 study conducted by the International Civil Aviation Organization (ICAO) on human resource development in Canada's aviation and aerospace industry provides a revealing glimpse into the challenges of workforce management in this sector, not just in Canada, but also worldwide.

One of the most alarming revelations was the aging demographic of the workforce, with troubling predictions that by 2017, around 40 percent of pilots and aircraft maintenance workers would be over the age of 65. This scenario indicated an impending wave of retirements, potentially leading to a significant gap in experienced personnel.

In 2006, the total count of the workforce in this sector stood at 141,000. However, due to attrition, there was a noticeable shortfall in effective manpower. Looking ahead, the study estimated that by 2017, the industry would need about 200,000 workers to meet its operational requirements efficiently, pointing towards a substantial shortage of 152,000 skilled workers. Breaking down this figure, the annual shortfall was projected to be around 12,000 skilled workers each year for the next 12 years, highlighting an urgent need for accelerated training and recruitment.

The implications of these findings are extensive and multifaceted. There is an immediate need to enhance training and education programs in aviation, covering not just pilots but also maintenance staff, air traffic controllers, and other critical aviation roles. Additionally, the industry must develop strategies to retain older, more experienced workers while facilitating the transfer of their knowledge and expertise to the younger workforce. Thankfully the Federal Aviation Administration has taken note and recently relaxed the mandatory retirement age from 60 to 65 years old.

While the study focused on Canada, its findings are globally relevant, as many countries face similar workforce challenges in aviation. This situation calls for a combined effort in leveraging technology and innovation to improve aviation operations and reduce the labor intensity. Moreover, governments and aviation authorities are urged to establish supportive policies and regulatory frameworks that encourage investment in human resource development and technological advancements in the field.

ICAO's study on human resource development in aviation highlights a critical juncture for the sector. With a looming shortage of skilled aviation professionals, the industry faces significant challenges. However, this also opens doors for innovation, improved training methodologies, and international collaboration to ensure the sustainable growth of the aviation industry.

The Rule of 72 and Its Implications in Aviation

The Rule of 72 is a simple yet powerful tool used in finance to estimate the time required for an investment to double in value at a fixed annual rate of interest. This rule states that by dividing 72 by the annual rate of growth, one can approximate the number of years it will take for the initial amount to double, based on compounding interest calculations. In the context of the aviation industry, this rule can be applied to understand the growth dynamics and the accompanying infrastructural demands.

So for example, as the aviation sector grows at an annual rate of about 4.3 percent, using the Rule of 72, we calculate that it would take roughly 16.74 years (72 divided by 4.3) for the industry to double in size. This doubling encompasses not just the number of aircraft and flights but also the overall industry infrastructure, including airports, maintenance facilities, and air traffic control systems.

So even a modest increase in passenger volume every year, say by 1 percent, adds significant pressure to scale up infrastructure. For instance, a 1 percent increase in passenger volume compounded annually translates to a substantial increase over a decade. Looking at the numbers a small 1 percent change in the increase in passenger volume, means that infrastructure has to be in 12 years not 14.4 years, thus shortening the time for your volume to double. When considering the cumulative effect over several years, especially in high-growth regions, this places a significant burden on existing aviation infrastructure.

Annual Increase in Passenger Volume	Number of Years for the Industry to Double
3%	24 years
4%	18 years
5%	14.4 years
6%	12 years
7%	10.2 years
8%	9 years
9%	8 years

This exponential growth not only challenges the physical infrastructure but also strains human resources in the industry. The need for trained professionals such as pilots, air traffic controllers, and maintenance staff escalates accordingly. For instance, a 4.3 percent annual growth in aviation operations would demand a parallel increase in workforce and expertise, which is currently not being met.

Okay, so to recap: the Rule of 72 provides a clear perspective on how swiftly the aviation industry is expanding and underscores the urgency to address the infrastructure and manpower requirements. Without timely and adequate responses to these growth rates, the industry might struggle to maintain efficiency and safety standards, which are paramount in aviation. It is, therefore, imperative for stakeholders to plan and invest in infrastructure and human resources proactively, considering these growth projections so as to keep up with aviation growth.

The Financial Hurdle of Becoming a Pilot

Choosing a career in aviation, particularly as a pilot, has always been a dream for many. However, the path to the cockpit or other aviation-related professions is increasingly becoming a steep financial challenge. The rising costs of pilot schools and other aviation educational facilities are becoming significant barriers for many aspiring professionals, impacting the diversity and accessibility of careers in this dynamic industry.

The journey to becoming a pilot is undeniably challenging, not only in terms of the rigor and dedication required but also due to the substantial financial investment it demands. Aspiring pilots face a steep uphill climb when it comes to financing their education and training, a hurdle that has grown more daunting over the years.

At the heart of the issue is the comprehensive nature of pilot training which is a combination of theoretical and practical exercises. This process encompasses a range of stages, starting from obtaining a private pilot license, advancing through various ratings and certifications, and culminating in a commercial pilot license. Each of these stages involves costs that are often underestimated at the outset.

The cost factors in pilot training are multifaceted. First and foremost, there are the direct costs associated with flight hours. Renting aircraft for training purposes is expensive, not just due to the rental rates but also because of the associated costs like fuel, maintenance, and insurance. Moreover, the training involves sophisticated flight simulators, which replicate real-world flying conditions but come with high usage fees.

In addition to flight training, there are classroom instruction fees. These classes cover a range of necessary topics, from navigation and meteorology to the technical aspects of flying different types of aircraft. The instructors themselves are highly trained professionals, and their expertise is reflected in the cost of the education provided.

The cumulative expense of obtaining a commercial pilot license can be comparable to that of a four-year college degree in the United States, often requiring students to take out substantial loans or seek other forms of financial support. For many, this financial burden is a significant barrier, deterring them from pursuing a career in aviation, despite having the passion and potential for it.

Furthermore, the investment does not stop once the initial training is complete. Pilots must continually invest in their training to keep their skills sharp and stay updated on the latest technologies and regulations. This requirement for ongoing education translates to additional expenses throughout a pilot's career.

Given all this, it's not surprising the financial hurdle of becoming a pilot is a complex and challenging aspect of the profession. This financial barrier not only affects individual aspirations but also has broader implications for the diversity and sustainability of the aviation workforce. Addressing this challenge is crucial for ensuring that the profession is accessible to talented individuals from all backgrounds.

These financial barriers can deter a diverse range of candidates from pursuing careers in aviation, leading to a shortage of skilled professionals in various areas of the industry. This shortage can have cascading effects on the efficiency, innovation, and safety of aviation operations. Furthermore, the lack of financial accessibility can lead to homogeneity within the workforce, depriving the industry of varied perspectives and innovative ideas that often come from a diverse talent pool.

Reduced Talent Pool and Industry Growth

The foremost impact of high educational costs narrows the talent pool. When the financial burden of training becomes prohibitive for a large segment of the population, the industry inevitably misses out on potentially skilled and passionate individuals. This limitation restricts the flow of new talent into the sector, which is especially concerning given the current and projected shortages of aviation professionals like pilots, air traffic controllers, and maintenance technicians.

A diverse workforce is a key driver of innovation. With financial barriers limiting the entry of a wide range of individuals, the industry risks a homogenized workforce that may lack in varied perspectives and creative solutions. This homogeneity can stifle innovation and reduce the competitiveness of the aviation sector in the global market. Diversity in the workforce not only brings different viewpoints but also fosters a culture of creativity and adaptability, which are crucial for the industry's growth and evolution.

Aviation is an inherently global industry, serving a diverse clientele across different cultures and regions. A workforce that reflects this diversity can better understand and cater to the varied needs and preferences of a global customer base. Financial barriers in aviation education, however, can impede this representation, leading to a workforce that may not fully comprehend or connect with the cultural nuances of its diverse clientele.

Implications for Safety and Standards

The financial barriers in aviation education and training also have profound long-term implications for safety and operational standards within the industry. These implications are critical, as the aviation sector is heavily reliant on skilled professionals to maintain its high safety standards.

Safety is paramount in aviation, and a skilled workforce is fundamental to maintaining it. The rigorous training and education required for aviation roles ensure that professionals are well-equipped to handle the complex and high-stakes situations they encounter. However, when financial barriers limit access to quality training, there's a risk of a less qualified workforce. This can lead to gaps in safety-critical knowledge and skills, which might compromise the safety standards the industry strives to uphold.

The aviation industry continually evolves its safety practices to keep pace with new technologies and changing environments. A diverse and well-trained workforce, brought about by accessible education, contributes significantly to this evolution. They bring fresh perspectives and innovative ideas essential for developing new safety protocols and improving existing ones. Financial constraints in education can hinder this influx of new talent and ideas, potentially slowing the pace of safety innovations.

The capacity of aviation professionals to respond to emergencies is a direct outcome of their training and expertise. In scenarios like equipment failures, adverse weather conditions, or security threats, the quality of response can be the difference between safety and catastrophe. Limited access to comprehensive training due to financial hurdles can weaken this critical response capacity, elevating risks in emergency situations.

Revolutionizing Recruitment and Training

So what is to be done? The industry is responding by reshaping its approach to recruitment and training. Accelerated training programs are being introduced to swiftly prepare new pilots and aviation technicians, maintaining high safety standards while reducing the time to workforce entry. Expanding recruitment to include underrepresented groups, such as women and minorities, is also key. This approach not only promotes diversity but also widens the talent pool. Furthermore, collaborations with universities and technical schools are forging pathways for tailored education that aligns with the industry's specific needs, ensuring a consistent flow of qualified graduates.

What about Millennials and Gen Z?

As the aviation industry evolves, it faces the critical task of appealing to the new workforce generations – Millennials and Generation Z. Known for valuing work-life balance, clear career progression, and opportunities to make a meaningful impact, these generations are reshaping the workplace. Airlines must, therefore, adapt their strategies to meet these new expectations and retain talented individuals from these cohorts.

Emphasizing Work-Life Balance

For starters, airlines can attract younger generations by offering flexible work arrangements. This could mean providing options for shift swapping, part-time roles, or even remote work for positions that allow it. Another significant draw is the focus on wellness programs. By prioritizing initiatives that address mental health, physical well-being, and stress management, airlines can demonstrate their commitment to the overall health of their employees, a key concern for Millennials and Gen Z.

Fostering Career Growth with Transparency

Clear and transparent career pathways are essential for Millennials and Gen Z, who seek to understand how they can grow within an organization. Airlines should ensure that career progression routes are well-defined and communicated. Additionally, replacing traditional annual reviews with continuous feedback, coupled with mentorship and ongoing training opportunities, can cultivate a culture of growth and support, aligning with the aspirations of these younger generations.

Professional development is another area where airlines can appeal to these generations. By offering extensive training programs, educational assistance, and opportunities to engage in diverse and challenging projects, airlines can satisfy the desire for personal and professional growth. Moreover, Millennials and Gen Z are often motivated by societal and environmental causes. Thus, airlines engaging in corporate social responsibility initiatives provide a platform for these employees to contribute to meaningful causes.

Airlines that understand and cater to the values and expectations of Millennials and Generation Z will be more successful in attracting and retaining talent from these groups. By creating a workplace that offers flexibility, clear growth paths, opportunities for development, and a chance to make a real-world impact, airlines can establish themselves as desirable employers for the younger workforce. Such adaptations not only secure a skilled and motivated workforce but also drive a culture of innovation and progress, which is vital for the aviation industry's continuous growth.

Embracing Technological Advancements

The integration of advanced simulation and virtual reality (VR) tools in training is a major leap forward. These technologies provide a highly realistic and immersive learning environment, allowing trainees to practice and hone their skills in a safe, controlled setting. For pilots, VR and simulation technologies can replicate a wide range of flight scenarios, from routine operations to emergency procedures, without the risk and cost associated with real-life training flights. This method of training is incredibly efficient, as it allows for repeated practice and immediate feedback, which is essential for skill mastery.

Embracing technology and innovation in the workplace is crucial to resonate with the tech-savvy Millennials and Gen Z. Utilizing the latest software and tools for workflow and communication can create an environment that is both efficient and appealing to younger employees. Additionally, leveraging social media and digital platforms for internal communication and community building can further engage these digitally native generations.

On the operational front, automation and artificial intelligence (AI) are playing a transformative role. In areas like baggage handling and check-in processes, the implementation of automated systems is significantly reducing the need for manual labor. For instance, automated baggage sorting systems can handle a high volume of luggage quickly and efficiently, minimizing delays and reducing the physical strain on staff.

AI-driven tools are being used to optimize flight schedules, crew assignments, and maintenance tasks, leading to more efficient operations. AI algorithms can analyze vast amounts of data to predict maintenance needs, thereby preventing equipment failures and reducing downtime. This not only improves operational efficiency but also enhances safety.

Impact on Workforce Requirements

By integrating these technological solutions, the aviation industry is able to do more with fewer staff, which is crucial in times of labor shortages. Moreover, this shift towards technology-driven operations requires a new set of skills from the workforce, leading to the creation of more specialized roles in IT, data analysis, and system maintenance within the aviation sector.

The aviation industry is undergoing a transformative phase in its approach to recruitment and training, responding innovatively to the critical need for more staff. This transformation is multi-faceted, focusing on not only increasing the quantity of recruits but also enhancing the quality and diversity of the workforce.

One of the key strategies being adopted is the introduction of accelerated training programs. These programs are designed to fast-track the education and certification process for new pilots and aviation technicians. The primary aim is to reduce the time it takes for trainees to become fully qualified, thus entering the workforce more quickly. However, this acceleration does not compromise safety standards, which remain a top priority. By streamlining the training process and focusing on essential skills and knowledge, these programs are efficiently preparing a new generation of aviation professionals.

Another critical aspect of the revamped recruitment strategy is the emphasis on diversity and inclusion. The aviation industry is expanding its recruitment efforts to include groups that have historically been underrepresented in the field, such as women and ethnic minorities. This move is not just about social responsibility; it's also a practical response to the staff shortage. By reaching out to a broader demographic, the industry taps into a wider pool of talent and perspectives, which can lead to more innovative solutions and a more inclusive work environment. This approach also helps in creating a workforce that reflects the diversity of the passengers and communities they serve.

Collaborations with Educational Institutions

Collaborations with universities and technical schools are also a crucial part of this new approach. These partnerships are creating specialized educational programs that are closely aligned with the needs of the aviation industry. By working together, the industry and educational institutions can ensure that the curriculum is relevant and up-to-date, equipping students with the skills and knowledge they need to succeed in modern aviation roles. These partnerships often include internships or cooperative education programs, allowing students to gain hands-on experience while they study, further preparing them for their future careers in aviation. Students get the opportunity to work within the industry, gaining invaluable hands-on experience that cannot be replicated in a classroom. These internships also allow students to apply their academic knowledge in practical settings, providing a clear understanding of the expectations and realities of working in aviation.

There are several noteworthy collaborations between airlines and educational institutions aimed at fostering the next generation of aviation professionals. For instance, Kent State University's College of Aeronautics and Engineering significantly benefited from a $6.5 million donation from FedEx, which allowed for the creation of a new academic center equipped with state-of-the-art aircraft simulators and classrooms. This investment has led to a substantial increase in enrollment and retention rates for the university's flight program.

Likewise, Delta Airlines and the Delta Lines Foundation have contributed to the development of a new aviation building at Auburn University, named the Delta Air Lines Aviation Education Building. FedEx has also offered $2.5 million in aviation scholarships across four universities.

Furthermore, Delta has established the Propel program in partnership with Kent State, providing a select group of students with an accelerated career track with the airline after graduation. This program currently includes 11 university partners and is expected to expand. Similarly, United have initiated training partnership programs like United's Aviate program, which collaborates with 18 universities to help train, mentor and recruit young pilots.

The Outcome

The result of these initiatives is a more efficient, diverse, and well-prepared workforce. With accelerated training, the industry is able to respond more quickly to the growing demand for professionals. By focusing on diversity, the industry not only becomes more inclusive but also more resilient and adaptable. And through educational partnerships, the industry ensures a steady supply of well-trained graduates ready to take on the challenges of modern aviation. Together, these efforts are setting a new standard in aviation recruitment and training, ensuring the industry's growth and sustainability in the years to come.

Last Thoughts

Addressing staff shortages also involves looking beyond national borders. Easing visa restrictions and facilitating international recruitment can help fill vacancies more rapidly. Additionally, advocating for government support in the form of funding, tax incentives, and streamlined certification processes can expedite workforce expansion.

The staff shortage in the aviation industry requires a blend of immediate and long-term strategies. By innovatively approaching recruitment, leveraging technology, valuing the existing workforce, and seeking global collaboration, the industry can effectively navigate these challenging times. The collaboration of all stakeholders in implementing these solutions is crucial, ensuring the sustainable development and resilience of the aviation sector.

Chapter 6:
The Role Of Commerce In Flight

Unlike other forms of transport, air transport offers unparalleled speed, making it the preferred choice for time-sensitive shipments such as perishable goods, high-value items, emergency supplies, and last-minute deliveries that are critical in the fast-paced world of commerce.

And as supply chains stretch across continents and become more integrated, the need for rapid transportation that can bridge vast distances has only become increasingly important. Manufacturers, retailers, and consumers increasingly rely on air cargo to ensure that products are moved swiftly from where they are made to where they are needed, often traversing multiple countries or continents.

Additionally, the incredible growth of e-commerce has transformed air cargo from a facilitator of global trade to an essential component of the retail ecosystem. Online shopping, with its promises of quick delivery times, has created a new demand for air cargo services. This is not just for international shipments, but also for domestic deliveries, where customers' expectations of 'same-day' or 'next-day' delivery options have become the norm. As a result, air cargo operators are constantly innovating to meet these increasing demands, investing in more efficient aircraft, better logistics planning, and advanced tracking systems to keep pace with the ever-evolving market requirements.

The History of Air Cargo

Let's first look back at the history of air cargo. For aviation lovers, it is actually a fascinating journey that mirrors the broader narrative of aviation and global commerce. Its inception can be traced back to the early 20th century, not long after the Wright brothers' first flight in 1903. Initially, the focus of using aircraft was primarily for mail transport, which marked the earliest form of air cargo.

The first scheduled air mail service began in 1918, operated by the United States Post Office. This service fundamentally changed the speed at which communication could happen across vast distances, setting the stage for the broader use of aircraft for cargo transport.

As aviation technology progressed rapidly through the 1920s and 1930s, the potential for air cargo began to expand beyond mail. The advent of larger and more reliable aircraft made it feasible to transport goods over longer distances.

After World War 2, the world witnessed a surge in international trade and a growing global economy. Air cargo started to play an increasingly vital role, facilitating faster trade across countries and continents. The introduction of jet aircraft in the 1950s further revolutionized the industry, drastically reducing travel times and increasing cargo capacities. This era marked the beginning of modern air cargo operations, with dedicated freighter aircraft and complex logistics networks starting to take shape.

Then in the latter part of the 20th century saw significant regulatory changes that further fuelled the growth of air cargo. The deregulation of the airline industry in several countries allowed for more competition and innovation in air cargo services. Airlines began to focus more on freight services, developing specialized cargo divisions and expanding their freighter fleets.

FedEx, founded by Frederick W. Smith, (initially named Federal Express) introduced the concept of overnight shipping—a novel idea at the time. Smith's vision was clear: a delivery service that could operate independently of traditional passenger routes and schedules, thus ensuring faster and more reliable deliveries.

FedEx's first night of operations was nothing short of monumental. On April 17, 1973, 14 small aircraft left Memphis, Tennessee, carrying 186 packages to 25 U.S. cities. This operation laid the groundwork for a logistics network that would eventually span the globe.

Technological advancements continued to be a driving force in the evolution of air cargo. The development of wide-body aircraft, such as the Boeing 747 in the 1970s, allowed for larger volumes of cargo to be transported, reducing costs and improving efficiency. Then the introduction of computerized tracking and logistics management systems revolutionized the way cargo was handled, tracked, and delivered, making the process more reliable and efficient.

Today, air cargo is an integral part of the global supply chain, characterized by a highly sophisticated and interconnected network of airlines, airports, logistics providers, and regulatory bodies. The industry continues to evolve, driven by new challenges and opportunities, such as the need for sustainable operations and the potential of emerging technologies like drones and autonomous aircraft.

Logistics and Operations in Air Cargo

The logistics and operations of air cargo encompass a range of activities that are vital for the efficient and safe transport of goods. This includes the critical processes of cargo handling and packaging, warehouse operations, and route planning, each playing a unique role in the overall system.

Packaging for air cargo must account for the stresses of air travel, such as changes in air pressure and temperature, as well as the risks of damage during loading and unloading. Specialized containers, known as 'Unit Load Devices' are often used to consolidate cargo and optimize space in the aircraft's cargo hold. These containers must be packed correctly to ensure the even distribution of weight, which is crucial for the safe operation of the aircraft. Additionally, cargo must be secured properly within these containers to prevent shifting during flight, which could potentially affect the aircraft's balance and performance.

Bimodal which involves the use of two different modes of transport - typically air and land - is becoming increasingly popular in our globalized economy. However, it brings with it a unique set of challenges, particularly when it comes to the interplay of different vehicle designs.

At the heart of these challenges is a simple, yet significant problem: the shape of transport vehicles. Trains and trucks, the stalwarts of land transportation, are predominantly designed with a square or rectangular profile. This design is optimized for maximizing space on the ground, where the horizontal plane is the primary area of concern.

Contrast this with aircraft, which are predominantly cylindrical or rounded in shape. This design is a product of aerodynamic requirements, where reducing air resistance is key to efficient flight. However, the rounded shape of an aircraft's cargo hold presents a stark contrast to the square containers or pallets typically used in trucks and trains.

Logistical Headaches

This discrepancy in design shapes leads to a host of logistical challenges. When transferring cargo from an aircraft to a truck or train (or vice versa), the mismatch in container shapes can result in inefficient use of space. This not only poses a problem in terms of cost but also impacts the environmental footprint of transportation. Inefficient space utilization means more trips, more fuel consumption, and, consequently, more emissions.

Moreover, the need to repack or rearrange goods for different modes of transport adds a layer of complexity in logistics management. It increases the time taken for goods to reach their destination and raises the risk of damage during handling.

Solutions and Innovations

Addressing these challenges requires innovative solutions. One approach is the development of specialized containers or pallets that can adapt to both rounded and square shapes. Another solution lies in improving logistics software to better plan and optimize the packing and routing of cargo.

Warehouse Operations

Warehouse operations are the next critical phase in the air cargo process. This involves the reception, storage, and dispatch of goods in a secure and efficient manner. Air cargo warehouses are equipped with advanced systems for inventory management, ensuring that cargo is tracked accurately throughout its journey. These warehouses are designed to accommodate a wide variety of cargo, including temperature-sensitive goods and hazardous materials, each requiring specialized storage solutions. The layout and organization of these facilities are optimized for quick and efficient handling, minimizing the time goods spend on the ground. This is particularly important in air cargo operations, where speed is a key factor. Security is also a major consideration in warehouse operations, with stringent measures in place to protect against theft, tampering, and other security threats.

Route Planning

Just like with passenger airlines, route planning in air cargo is a complex task that involves balancing numerous factors to determine the most efficient and cost-effective way to move goods. This includes considering the range and capacity of aircraft, fuel costs, weather conditions, air traffic, and regulatory restrictions.

Airlines and cargo operators use sophisticated software to plan routes, taking into account the dynamic nature of air travel and the need for flexibility in response to unexpected changes. Efficient route planning is crucial not only for on-time deliveries but also for minimizing operational costs and environmental impact. Additionally, in the context of global logistics networks, route planning often involves coordination with other modes of transport, ensuring seamless intermodal connections for door-to-door delivery services.

Skilled Workforce Needs in Air Cargo Operations

The efficiency and success of the air cargo industry are heavily dependent on a skilled workforce, capable of managing the complex and varied tasks that this sector demands. Alongside the advancements in technology, the human element remains crucial, requiring a blend of specialized skills and adaptability to the evolving nature of the industry.

Cargo handlers, for instance, are at the frontline of the operation, responsible for the physical handling of cargo, ensuring it is loaded and unloaded safely, efficiently, and in compliance with all regulatory requirements. Their work demands not only physical strength and stamina but also a keen understanding of safety procedures and handling techniques for a wide range of cargo types, including hazardous materials and fragile goods.

Logistics analysts play a pivotal role in orchestrating the complex journey of air cargo. They are responsible for designing and managing supply chain processes, optimizing routes, and ensuring cost-effective and timely delivery of goods. This role requires strong analytical skills, proficiency in logistics software, and the ability to solve problems creatively in a fast-paced environment.

Flight operations personnel, including pilots and flight engineers, are integral to the operation. Their expertise ensures that the aircraft are operated safely, efficiently, and in accordance with all flight regulations. They need to be highly skilled in aircraft systems, navigation, and have the ability to make critical decisions under pressure.

Impact of Technological Advancements on Workforce Skillsets

The rapid advancement of technology in the air cargo industry has significantly altered the skillsets required from its workforce. Automation and digitalization are transforming traditional roles, necessitating a higher level of technical proficiency across all areas of operation. For example, the increasing use of advanced tracking and logistics management software requires cargo handlers and logistics analysts to be adept in digital tools and data analysis.

The integration of technologies such as AI, robotics, and drones into cargo operations is creating new roles and responsibilities. Employees are now required to have a blend of traditional industry knowledge and cutting-edge technological skills. This includes understanding automated systems, managing unmanned aerial vehicles for cargo delivery, and leveraging AI for predictive analytics in logistics planning.

Furthermore, as the industry moves towards more sustainable practices, there is a growing need for expertise in green technologies and environmentally friendly logistics solutions. This shift is creating opportunities for innovation and requiring new skill sets focused on sustainability.

Pilots in Cargo Vs. Passenger Airlines

The role of a pilot in the cargo sector, when contrasted with that of a passenger airline pilot, presents a unique set of challenges and responsibilities that go beyond the basic skill of flying an aircraft. These differences span across various aspects of their job, from the nature of their flight schedules to the very dynamics of flying the aircraft.

Cargo pilots typically face irregular flight schedules. Unlike passenger airline pilots who often have more predictable flight patterns, cargo pilots need to adapt to flights that frequently occur at night. This is primarily to meet the stringent deadlines of shipping schedules, where timely delivery is crucial. Additionally, the routes they fly can be more varied than those of passenger flights. Cargo pilots sometimes find themselves charting courses to less common destinations such as Anchorage Alaska which, due to its location, is a huge cargo hub, but isn't much of a passenger destination. This variety requires cargo pilots to be adaptable and well-versed in navigating a diverse range of air routes and airports.

The handling and performance of cargo planes differ significantly from passenger aircraft, especially when they are heavily loaded. The weight and distribution of cargo can affect the aircraft's center of gravity, altering its handling characteristics, particularly during critical phases like take-off and landing. Cargo pilots must possess a deep understanding of these dynamics and be proficient in adjusting their flying techniques accordingly. This skill is crucial not just for the safety of the flight, but also to ensure the integrity of the cargo being transported by trains, ships, and trucks.

The diversity in cargo, from luxury cars, fresh flowers, pharmaceuticals, and even high-value items like diamonds, presents a unique set of challenges for those in the transportation industry. Each type of cargo requires different handling procedures, security measures, and transport conditions. It's a world where precision, expertise, and sometimes a bit of creativity is crucial.

For those working in cargo transport, this variety can be both challenging and rewarding. There's a certain thrill in knowing that you're responsible for safely delivering something as precious as a crate of diamonds or as essential as emergency relief supplies.

In terms of interpersonal dynamics, cargo pilots typically experience less interaction compared to their counterparts in passenger airlines. The absence of passengers and limited contact with flight and ground crew can lead to a more solitary experience. However, this aspect of the job requires cargo pilots to be comfortable with working independently and being more self-reliant.

Understanding the weight and balance of the aircraft is another critical aspect for cargo pilots. Unlike passenger planes where weight distribution is relatively predictable, cargo aircraft can carry a wide variety of goods, each with different weights and sizes. Pilots must be skilled in assessing how the cargo's loading affects the aircraft's overall performance and stability. This knowledge is essential not only for safe flight but also for efficient fuel consumption and optimal aircraft handling.

The change in air cargo and e-commerce hasn't only effected pilots, of course. A wide range of employees may need to reskill or upskill to stay relevant in the changing job landscape. For instance, traditional cargo handlers might need training in automated systems, or require additional knowledge in e-commerce operations and digital communication platforms. Airlines and logistics companies must invest in training programs to help their workforce adapt to these new technologies and processes.

The Role of Technology in Air Cargo

Technology has played a pivotal role, revolutionizing the way goods are transported across the globe. The emergence of tracking systems, automation, and the profound impact of e-commerce, particularly the rise of Amazon, have reshaped the industry in ways that were unimaginable a few decades ago. Amazon's entry into the air cargo domain has been both transformative and disruptive, altering the traditional dynamics of the industry.

The integration of advanced tracking systems has been a game-changer in air cargo logistics. These systems provide real-time data on cargo location and status, greatly enhancing transparency and efficiency. Automation, too, has streamlined operations, from warehouse management to flight scheduling, reducing human error and operational costs.

The most significant technological impact, however, has come from the e-commerce boom, led by Amazon. E-commerce has not only increased the volume of goods transported via air but also heightened customer expectations for faster delivery times. This has compelled the air cargo industry to innovate continuously to keep pace with the rapidly changing demands.

Amazon's Disruptive Influence on Air Cargo

Like so many other industries, Amazon has played a pivotal role in changing how air transportation operates and has been a major disruptive force. Initially reliant on traditional carriers for its massive shipping needs, Amazon shifted gears by launching its own air cargo service, Amazon Air. This move towards controlling more of its logistics chain was a strategic decision to meet the growing demands of its e-commerce platform, ensuring faster and more reliable delivery to customers.

Amazon's approach has been multifaceted – acquiring a fleet of cargo planes, investing in advanced logistics infrastructure, and developing sophisticated tracking and automation systems. This aggressive expansion has not only provided Amazon with greater control over its shipping operations but has also posed a significant challenge to traditional air cargo carriers and logistics companies.

The landscape of air cargo has been significantly reshaped by technological advancements and the seismic impact of e-commerce, particularly by Amazon. The story of Amazon Air is not just about innovation but also a reflection of the company's relentless pursuit to fulfill its customer-centric promises, even in the face of operational crises.

The Birth of Amazon Air

Amazon's journey into developing its own air network stemmed from a crucial period of logistical challenges. Back in 2013, the company faced a critical situation that threatened its core promise of timely delivery, especially during the holiday season. A significant portion of Amazon's packages had failed to reach customers on time, primarily due to ground transportation issues. This failure was deeply troubling for a company built on Jeff Bezos' doctrine of customer obsession. The prospect of repeating this failure was not an option for Amazon's executives.

Amazon recognized that the company's dependence on external carriers like FedEx and UPS, particularly for air transport, was a critical vulnerability. Amazon needed more control over its delivery network to prevent future crises and uphold its Prime commitment of two-day shipping.

The decision to establish its own air network was a bold move by Amazon, driven by the necessity to have greater control over its delivery operations. Scott Ruffin, an ex-marine logistics officer, played a pivotal role in this transition. He started out helping to charter planes to ensure timely delivery of products, salvaging the holiday season. But this was a temporary fix. Amazon's long-term strategy was to build a robust air cargo service under its direct control. The company moved quickly to build its fleet, a mix of owned and leased aircraft, operated by various air carriers. This rapid development was a testament to Amazon's ability to innovate and scale operations swiftly. One of the key initiatives was the company's $1.5 billion investment in a hub at Cincinnati/Northern Kentucky International Airport, a clear indicator of its commitment to building a formidable presence in air cargo.

However, the creation of Amazon Air has not been without its challenges and criticisms. The aviation industry, known for its slow pace due to factors like stringent government regulations and the high cost of operations, posed a stark contrast to Amazon's rapid innovation culture. Balancing the operational demands of air cargo with safety, labor relations, and security compliance was a complex undertaking.

The Pros and Cons of Amazon's Entry into Air Cargo

The entry of Amazon into the air cargo sector has both positive and negative implications in the aviation industry. On the one hand, it has spurred innovation within the industry. Amazon's emphasis on speed and efficiency has led to advancements in logistics technology and practices, benefiting the industry as a whole. Moreover, it has created new jobs and opportunities in the logistics and aviation sectors.

On the other hand, Amazon's dominance raises concerns. Its vast resources and control over large portions of the supply chain could potentially squeeze out smaller players, reducing competition. There are also worries about the long-term effects on the industry if Amazon continues to expand its reach and influence.

Air Cargo Industry Response to Amazon's Rise

Amazon's entry into the air cargo industry with Amazon Air marked a significant shift in the dynamics of the sector. This move not only showcased Amazon's commitment to controlling its logistics but also posed a challenge to established players like FedEx, UPS, and other transportation companies. The response of these traditional carriers and competitors has been multifaceted, reflecting the evolving landscape of global logistics and e-commerce.

Adaptation and Strategic Shifts by FedEx and UPS

FedEx and UPS, long-standing giants in the air cargo industry, have had to reassess their strategies in light of Amazon's aggressive expansion. FedEx, in a bold move, terminated its Amazon contracts in 2019. This decision was part of a broader strategy to focus on the broader e-commerce market rather than depend on a single major customer. By distancing itself from Amazon, FedEx aimed to diversify its client base and avoid potential conflicts of interest as Amazon grew its own logistics capabilities.

UPS, on the other hand, has continued to work with Amazon while simultaneously strengthening its own network to better serve a growing and diverse e-commerce sector. UPS has invested heavily in automation, upgraded its aircraft fleet, and expanded its global reach to ensure faster and more efficient service. This approach reflects a dual strategy of catering to the immediate demand from Amazon's business while also building resilience against potential future competition.

Responses from Other Cargo Carriers

Beyond FedEx and UPS, other cargo carriers and logistics companies have also responded to Amazon's growing presence in the air cargo sector. Many have accelerated their investments in technology to improve tracking, efficiency, and customer service. There's been a notable increase in partnerships and alliances within the industry, as companies seek to pool resources and expertise to compete more effectively against Amazon's scale.

Smaller regional carriers, in particular, have found opportunities in niches that larger carriers or Amazon might not efficiently serve. These companies often focus on specialized cargo services or target specific geographic areas, offering personalized and flexible services that larger companies may not provide.

Innovation and Diversification

The industry's response to Amazon's entry has not been limited to defensive strategies. Many companies are exploring innovative solutions to stay competitive. This includes experimenting with drone deliveries, investing in electric and more environmentally friendly aircraft, and exploring new business models like on-demand cargo services.

Diversification has also become a key theme. Companies are expanding their services beyond air cargo, offering integrated logistics solutions that include ground transportation, warehousing, and supply chain management. This holistic approach is designed to provide end-to-end solutions to customers, making them less reliant on any single mode of transport or service.

Comparing Air Transportation with Passenger Airlines

The air cargo industry, while sharing some similarities with passenger airlines, faces its own unique set of challenges. These challenges, including capacity and demand fluctuations, as well as infrastructure constraints, differ in significant ways from those encountered by passenger airlines. Understanding these differences is key to appreciating the complexities of air cargo operations.

One of the primary challenges in air cargo is managing the balance between capacity and demand. Unlike passenger airlines, where demand can be relatively predictable and stable, (not counting once-in-a-lifetime events like COVID) air cargo demand is often volatile and influenced by various factors like global trade trends, economic policies, and economic cycles. For example, demand for air cargo services can spike dramatically during peak shopping seasons like the holidays or drop suddenly during economic downturns.

Infrastructure Constraints

Infrastructure constraints present significant challenges for both air cargo and passenger airlines, but the nature of these challenges can differ. Airports are often designed with passenger traffic as the priority, which can lead to limitations in cargo handling capacities and facilities. Cargo operations require specialized infrastructure, such as large warehouse spaces, cargo handling equipment, and dedicated areas for sorting and storing different types of cargo, including hazardous materials or perishables.

While passenger airlines also face challenges with airport infrastructure, such as the need for adequate gates and passenger terminals, the specific requirements for cargo operations are distinct. For instance, cargo carriers often need access to airports with longer runways to accommodate larger freighter aircraft and facilities for customs clearance and security screening specific to cargo.

Demand and Infrastructure Similarities

There are, however, some similarities in the challenges faced by both sectors. Both air cargo and passenger airlines are impacted by broader economic and geopolitical factors, such as trade wars, fuel price fluctuations, and global economic conditions. Additionally, both sectors are subject to regulatory changes and environmental policies that can affect operational efficiencies and costs.

Both types of airlines also grapple with the need for modernizing infrastructure to keep pace with technological advancements and increasing demands. This includes the implementation of advanced tracking and management systems, the adoption of more efficient and sustainable aircraft, and the need to enhance overall operational efficiency.

Intermodal Transportation Integration in Air Cargo

Intermodal transportation uses different types of transport to move cargo from origin to destination and plays a crucial role in the air cargo industry. This integration with other transport methods, such as road, rail, and sea, is essential for the efficient and seamless movement of goods. However, it also presents unique challenges alongside its benefits.

Air cargo often forms a part of a longer logistics chain that includes ground and sometimes sea transportation. For instance, goods may be transported by truck from a manufacturing facility to an airport, flown to another country, and then moved by rail or road to their final destination. This integration is vital for the global supply chain, as it allows for the swift movement of goods over long distances by air, combined with the cost-effectiveness and accessibility of ground or sea transport for shorter distances or areas not serviced by air.

The connection between these modes, unsurprisingly, involves careful coordination and timing. Cargo needs to be transferred seamlessly between different transport methods, requiring synchronized schedules and efficient handling operations. This is where sophisticated logistics management systems come into play, ensuring that transitions between modes are smooth and that delays are minimized.

One of the major challenges of intermodal transport is the need for coordination among different carriers and logistics providers. Each mode of transport operates under different regulations, has its own scheduling challenges, and requires specific handling procedures. Therefore, ensuring a seamless transition of cargo between these modes demands high levels of operational efficiency and communication.

Infrastructure compatibility is another challenge. Facilities like ports, rail terminals, and airports must be equipped to handle intermodal transfers, which include the need for adequate storage, appropriate loading and unloading equipment, and connectivity to other transport networks.

Additionally, tracking and visibility of cargo across different modes can be complex. Maintaining a continuous flow of information about the cargo's location and condition requires advanced tracking systems that are compatible across various transport modes.

Benefits of Intermodal Transport

Despite these challenges, intermodal transportation offers significant benefits. It provides flexibility in choosing the most efficient and cost-effective route and mode of transport for each segment of a shipment's journey. This can lead to reduced transportation costs and improved access to different markets.

Environmental benefits are also notable. By combining modes effectively, it's possible to reduce the carbon footprint of transportation. For instance, using rail for long land distances instead of trucks can significantly decrease fuel consumption and emissions.

Moreover, intermodal transport can enhance cargo security. By reducing the number of cargo handlings and using secure intermodal containers, the risk of damage and theft can be minimized.

Global Trade Dynamics in Air Cargo

The air transportation industry is intricately linked to global trade dynamics, with trade routes, economic corridors, and international trade agreements playing significant roles in shaping its operations. Understanding these factors is crucial in comprehending the complex nature of air cargo logistics and its susceptibility to global economic shifts.

Major air transportation routes typically connect manufacturing hubs with key consumer markets. For instance, routes from East Asia to North America and Europe are among the busiest, reflecting the flow of goods from manufacturing centers in countries like China and South Korea to large consumer markets in the West. These economic corridors, such as the New Silk Road, which is a loosely defined geographic location in central Asia, and includes both land and maritime routes connecting Asia with Europe, have significant implications for air cargo. These corridors are clusters of economic activities, including manufacturing zones, logistics hubs, and trade ports which influence the volume and type of cargo being transported, necessitating air cargo operators to strategically position their services to tap into these busy trade flows.

Impact of Trade Agreements and Tariffs

Then there are international trade agreements and tariffs which have a direct impact on the air cargo industry. Agreements that facilitate free trade, such as NAFTA (now replaced by the United States-Mexico-Canada Agreement or USMCA), can increase the volume of goods transported as they reduce trade barriers between countries. Similarly, regional trade agreements in Europe, Asia, and other parts of the world can stimulate air cargo traffic by easing cross-border movement of goods.

Conversely, tariffs and trade wars can disrupt air cargo operations. For example, the U.S.-China trade dispute in recent years led to fluctuations in air cargo volumes, as tariffs affected the movement of goods like electronics and machinery between the two countries. Such disputes can force air cargo carriers to adjust their capacity and routes in response to changing trade flows.

And, of course, trade policies and world politics can influence the cost structure of air cargo. Tariffs on aviation-related goods, such as aircraft parts or fuel, can increase operational costs for air cargo carriers, potentially affecting freight rates and service offerings.

The Future of Air Transportation

E-commerce has irrevocably altered the landscape of the air freight industry. In the wake of the global pandemic, a seismic shift occurred in consumer behavior, with a marked increase in online shopping. This surge has placed unprecedented demands on the air transportation sector, a trend that shows no signs of letting up.

As consumer expectations evolve and technology advances, the need for more efficient transportation will only grow stronger. The companies that recognize and adapt to this shift will be the ones leading the charge into a new era of air freight. This will mean more jobs for everyone in the aviation field. As the industry becomes more complex and interconnected, there will be a greater need for strategic roles. This includes managers who can oversee the integration of e-commerce into existing aviation models, strategists to navigate the evolving market landscape, and logistics experts who can optimize supply chain efficiency.

Chapter 7:
Pilot Careers

If I were a betting man, I would probably guess that you've dreamed of becoming a pilot ever since you could remember. You probably used to play with toy airplanes, taxing them down the imaginary runway, and then taking off, imagining you pulling back the throttle, going faster...climbing higher, flying over the other toys, chairs, tables.

Becoming a pilot is one of those dream jobs—right up there with being a rock musician, a surgeon, and the CEO of a Silicon Valley tech company. If you are truly serious about being a pilot, you, of course, know it takes many hours of training, studying, and practice to become a pilot. It's a converted job by many. In this chapter, we'll dive into everything that you need to know about what it takes to make it as a pilot.

The Need for Pilots

There are several reasons that drive the need for pilots, including rapid globalization, rising national and domestic incomes, the emergence of low-cost carriers, and technological improvements. As the globe becomes more and more interconnected, conducting business globally has become more accessible than ever with the emergence of e-commerce and online shopping. Now, it is even easier for B-to-B business relationships to develop and for international businesses to deliver products to the end user. Rising incomes within numerous global regions have increased the demand for air transportation services in the business, vacation, and friends and family travel markets. Airlines have expanded their routes, developed strategic solid alliances and codeshares, and delivered products that appeal to all income levels. This product line includes economy travel, premium economy, and first-class travel.

Pilots and Low-cost Carriers (LCC)

We've talked about how LCCs have fundamentally changed the structure of airline operations and branding to make air travel even more accessible to the public. Such strategies include one cabin class configuration and one fair type with limited flexibility. The "Buy on Board" snack bar reduces the catering cost and adds another income stream: advertising labels posted on the backs of seats, overhead bins, and in-flight magazines. One aircraft type fleet configuration reduces operational costs, and point-to-point operations mean a simplified operation, thus reducing operating costs.

In addition, LCC airlines save on operational costs by eliminating a grooming team. Flight Attendants and Pilots must groom the aircraft between flight legs during the day. The inflight uniform design is not custom designed but rather an assembly of items from a generic uniform supply company with a unique scarf or tie. LCC avoid operating flights out of major hubs but prefer smaller airports with lower operating costs, may choose departure/arrival times that are less desirable and therefore more economical, and choose to park the aircraft on hard stands rather than at jetways, which are more convenient for passengers but also more expensive.

While trying to predict the future is dicey at best, LCC operations are here to stay and provide an essential role in the aviation industry, keeping the sector, as a whole, more competitive, which means more jobs all around.

Technological Improvements

Technological improvements allow aircraft to fly further with less fuel consumption, thus reducing the overall cost of travel. In addition, enhanced aerodynamic features, such as winglet design and the composite material of the aircraft, further reduce the aircraft's overall weight. Navigation and communication have also helped reduce travel time and cost of travel, making it more accessible to the masses.

Disposable Family Income

Increase Disposable family income related to the GDP. As the GDP increases in many regions, so does the disposable family income. Therefore, the general population has the funds to travel. According to the O.E.C.D., the global economic outlook is for a 2.7 to 2.9 percent GDP increase. Not all regions of the world will have the same growth rate. India has the highest growth rate of 6 percent, followed by China at 5.4 percent, and in third place is Indonesia, with a 4.7 percent increase in GDP As family income increases, so does the capability to afford airfares. This will increase the demand for air travel in those regions and select routes. In addition, it will push airport infrastructure under extreme pressure to accommodate this added demand.

The Effects of Aircraft Ordering

Larger aircraft, such as the Boeing 747 and the Airbus 380, will require fewer pilots to transport 100,000 between two points. This option is profitable for the airline but not so convenient for the passengers. Alternatively, single-aisle aircraft such as the Airbus 320 or 321 Neo L.R. will require more pilots to transport the same number of passengers, allowing for more travel options and route planning flexibility.

If an airline transports 100,000 passengers between two cities, choosing an Airbus 321 LR or an Airbus 380 will directly affect the number of pilots required to complete this task.

Airbus 380	100,000 / 550 = 182 flights X 2 = 364 pilots
Airbus 321 LR	100,000 / 240 = 417 flights X 2 = 833 pilots

From the simple calculation above, we can see that if an airline modifies its fleet from an Airbus 380 to an Airbus 321 on a given route, there is a direct increase in the number of pilots required to transport the same number of passengers. Airbus has over 5400 orders for the Airbus 321 Neo and only 251 orders for the Airbus 380 as of August 2023.

For example, flying with one aircraft from Toronto to London is more efficient and cost-effective. However, from a passenger perspective, it is more convenient to have more options. Passengers may prefer two options to cross the Atlantic Ocean, one from Halifax to Birmingham and one from Montreal to London, Gatwick. This strategy allows for two points of origin and two different European destinations. However, the cockpit crew is double. As airlines opt to purchase the Airbus 320 Neo L.R., it will open up these route options between long haul flights and medium-sized airports globally, therefore driving the need for pilot demand. New pilots who understand what drives the industry will find it easier to forge a career path and find higher paying job openings.

As older pilots retire, new opportunities arise for younger pilots. New pilots often take on less desirable jobs to accumulate the necessary flight hours for better positions.

As COVID-19 was dismantling the aviation infrastructure, any hope of recovery would be many years away. However, by 2022, passenger volume return, and in 2023, many airlines, routes, and airports have returned to 85 percent of pre-COVID traffic volume. Recent studies show that more than the pilot supply will be needed to meet the demand by 2024 and will continue to worsen as the years and decades progress. The pilot shortage is most acutely felt in the United States. However, other countries will follow as decades progress.

Global pilot demand versus supply
2020-2032, end of year

What Are the Core Reasons For The Surge in Pilot Demand?

The answer is complex. What is the current demand for each region globally? What is the age bell curve of pilots in each focus group, and what is the number of years to retirement? How many pilots may consider "an exodus" or "pilot brain drain"?

There is also a gender imbalance within the pilot workforce. 94 percent of pilots are male, while 6 percent are female. The reason for this imbalance is related to the fact that a pilot career is a S.T.E.M. (Science, Technology, Engineering, and Math) related field. The number of pilots who commute to work in another country. How aggressively are local pilot schools marketing their programs to meet the future national demand? Funding to develop pilot training at national, provincial, and local levels will also stimulate enrollment in pilot training programs. Finally, overcoming financial barriers to completing the training programs will also boost enrollment numbers.

Even though COVID-19 temporarily altered the demand for pilots and other aviation professionals, studies show that the fundamental market remains unchanged. The C.A.E. states that 260,000 new pilots are required in the next ten years (C.A.E.). This continued increase in pilot demand raises the question of how each country will retain its pilot workforce and prevent a pilot brain drain.

Pilot Staffing

Aircraft typically require two pilots. While many aircraft can take off, cruise, and land on autopilot, passengers are reluctant to travel in an aircraft with one pilot, not to mention completely autonomous aircraft. Therefore, in the foreseeable future, pilots will continue to be required on all commercial flights. It is doubtful that airlines can replace a pilot with someone with no experience because, in an emergency, the lack of experience could cause the complete loss of the aircraft and the lives on board the aircraft. This raises the question of how to conduct career marketing for a pilot, select potential pilots, and motivate new pilots. Studies show that 40 percent of pilots will retire in the next seven years.

Understanding the supply and demand for pilots and putting it in the global market context for aviation professionals is essential. H.T. News Desk states that Pieter Elbers, C.E.O. of Indigo Airlines, placed an order for 500 Airbus 320 Neo. With a list price of $55 billion, the deal is the highest civil aviation in history. India is outpacing Canada with their aircraft orders. Air Canada has 200 aircraft and has recently added 19 new aircraft to its fleet to meet surging demand for pilots. It is easy to see that other regions of the world are outpacing the growth of Canada's aviation industry.

Pilots' Association

According to the Air Line Pilots Association (A.L.P.A.), the industry has produced enough pilots to meet current demand. However, these numbers relate to the United States of America and not other regions of the world.

As COVID-19 was dismantling the aviation infrastructure, any hope of recovery would be many years away. However, by 2022 passenger volume return, and in 2023, many airlines, routes, and airports will have returned to 85 percent of pre-COVID traffic volume. Recent studies show that more than the pilot supply will be needed to meet the demand by 2024 and will continue to worsen as the years and decades progress. The pilot shortage is most acutely felt in the United States. However, other countries will follow as decades progress.

Based on the information above and strong industry trends, over the next 20 years, the pilot supply and demand will be felt the strongest in China, India, the United States, and the Middle East. Countries offering better compensation and more favorable work conditions will be able to attract pilots from around the world. A quick overview of the supply and demand of pilots in each country will be insightful.

Pilot Demand Forecasting in China

A study conducted in 2022 at the Shanghai University of Engineering stated that the State Council predicted that China would need 5,000 aircraft by 2020. However, by December 2020, the total aircraft count was

2,461. The reason cited for this shortage was simply a lack of pilot supply. The article mentions that to boost the pilot workforce, pilot schools and colleges would need to be set up to train pilots to meet the demand over the next 5 to 15 years.

Pilot Demand Forecasting in India

"Airbus estimates that the 'propensity of travel' in India is 0.1 per capita per year, forecasted to increase to 0.4 per capita per year by 2037. This four-fold increase does not factor in general aviation, helicopters, aerial work, and cargo. India is at the cusp of explosive growth in air travel domestically and internationally within Asia and other international destinations. Market watchers will note that all airlines in India are gradually shifting their focus and placing orders for long-range/wide-body aircraft. Initiatives by the Government of India - U.D.A.N. - Regional Connectivity Scheme are designed to make air travel convenient, accessible, and cost-effective for people.

These new schemes act as an impetus for airlines, and several large orders with manufacturers have been placed and will continue to be placed. The 2019 Boeing Pilot & Technician Outlook, a respected industry forecast of personnel demand, projects that 804,000 new civil aviation pilots will be needed to fly over the next 20 years. The forecast includes the commercial aviation, corporate aviation, and civil helicopter industries. The Asia Pacific region will lead the worldwide growth in demand for pilots, with a requirement for 266,000 new pilots.

Pilot Demand Forecasting in The United States

Many organizations monitor the pilot supply and demand in their jurisdiction. The Federal Aviation Authority (F.A.A.) manages the issuance of pilot licenses in the United States. Pilot Institute studies the supply and demand for pilots in the United States and makes this comment.

"The total number of pilots includes both student pilots and for-hire pilots. From the tally of student pilots, it is easy to see that most of them are on the younger side – around 21 percent belong to the 20 to 29 age group, and around 18 percent are aged 30 to 39. This is not surprising, as most pilots get their training at a young age. The high numbers may also provide a false assurance, as it is pretty much a given that not all these students will develop into for-hire pilots.

To give us a more realistic perspective of the status of the current pilot population, we must look at the total number of for-hire pilots. The shift is massive. Based on the data, more than 30 percent of the current for-hire pilots fall within the age range of 50 to 64. In 2009, the U.S. Congress changed the mandatory retirement age of airline pilots from 60 to 65 to solve the pilot shortage problem. This means that around 30 percent of the for-hire pilots we have right now will have to retire within the next 15 years.

The facts become even more sobering when you take the total number of for-hire pilots in the 50 to 64 age group. The total is about 150,000 pilots. Suppose we live in an ideal world where all student pilots convert into for-hire pilots after they finish the training and certification process. To make up for the population of pilots who will retire in the next 15 years, we will need all student pilots in the age range of 16 to 54 to become for-hire pilots. To compare further, the number of student pilots aged 20 to 39 is only around 113,000."

Pilot Demand Forecasting in the Middle East

According to global consultancy management company Oliver Wyman, as the aviation industry recovers from the global pandemic, the Middle East will feel the effects of the pilot shortage the most outside the United States. The pilot supply and demand coincide with flat, followed by a dropping supply of pilots in the region, in addition to the lay-offs related to COVID-19 and, at the same, the lack of enrolment in the pilot training programs.

"If demand for air travel continues to grow, airlines need to accelerate recruiting efforts from other regions where we anticipate less acute shortages, particularly Latin America and Asia Pacific, to fill gaps. Failing that, we may see adjusting schedules into and out of the region, impacting the Middle East's carriers and airport operators," says Andre Martins, who is a partner and the Head of Transportation, Services and Operations at Oliver Wyman.

"Oliver Wyman forecasted in early 2021 that an impending pilot shortage was on the horizon, contrary to reality at the time, as COVID-19 was decimating the airline industry and any recovery appeared years away. We are now predicting global aviation to be short nearly 80,000 pilots by 2032, absent a downturn in future demand or air travel and strenuous efforts by the industry to bolster the supply of pilots."

However, the Middle East is home to some of the wealthiest countries in the world, so their national airlines, most of which are government owned and have deep pockets, will likely just increase the wages of pilots, enticing many younger pilots from North America and Europe away from jobs in their home country.

Pilot Demand Forecasting in Asia

Bringing together the above situation and its complexities, China and India face the most significant pilot shortage due to an increase in new aircraft acquisition and an unstoppable demand based on their large population pools with the economic capability to purchase airfares. The aviation industry in the United States has reached maturity, with established infrastructure and a strong demand for air transportation services; however, within the next ten years, many pilots will retire. The U.S. Congress has already intervened by expanding the retirement age for pilots from 60 to 65. The Middle East also faces a pilot shortage, but they are the wealthiest countries in this region. Therefore, they can lure pilots from overseas to fill the pilot gap. This creates the "perfect storm," where recruit pilots from Canada may consider relocating overseas for better wages and work conditions.

Canada's Position in The Global Pilot Supply and Demand.

In Canada, Transport Canada regulates the transportation industry, including aviation, and the required licenses. Since the pandemic, Transport Canada has continued monitoring aviation retirement, growth rates, and industry demand. Transport Canada also recognized many barriers to entry into this career path, including financial barriers, permanent residency status, and progressive practical and theoretical exams. Transport Canada is also working with Foreign Affairs Canada and Immigration, Refugee, and Citizenship Canada (I.R.C.C.) to facilitate foreign workers to get the necessary documents to progress in this career.

The report that Transport Canada (T.C.) issued on February 15, 2023, acknowledges that more than Canadian students alone will be needed to fill the gap required to meet industry demand. Transport Canada (T.C.) also identifies that capital investment is a significant barrier for students to start or complete their pilot licenses. As a result, T.C. is actively collaborating with Employment and Social Development Canada to facilitate student loans and pilot program training.

The Pilot Career Path

Prospective pilot students enroll in flight school and pass successive theoretical and practical exams. Flight schools will enroll only enough students to fill their aircraft and instructor rosters. However, a single flight school may need more oversight and the ability to respond to the needs of the industry. Prominent airlines, such as Air Canada, will hire from subsidiary airlines, such as Air Canada Rouge. Canadian Charter Airlines will lease from SunWing Airlines or Nordair. The smaller airlines will hire directly from the flight schools. Pilot training is very technical and is a career that is highly regulated, which requires many flight hours and certification.

A pilot needs to be STEM-minded. They need to like math and calculations. They will not be a good pilot if they do not like that. They require around $80,000 to $100,000 in funding to complete the pilot license and 3 to 4 years of study to commit to completing the training program—mentorship, good weather, budget, and about 200 hours of flight school.

They require support from the family, the school, and the employer. They may need to relocate to a remote area to complete their hours. Typically, the candidate will start with a local or regional airline to further build their hours, then progress to a larger national airline and progress from First Officer to Captain.

The irregular hours and frequent travel can be challenging, especially for those with families. And to make things more chaotic, a pilot's work hours are often irregular and dependant on the weather. In northern regions, pilots often risk their lives completing operational demands and put themselves, the aircraft, cargo, and passengers in danger. The constant changes in altitude and cabin pressure can be overcome. One always needs to be vigilant for early signs of hypoxia.

Every country has its aviation authority with specific pilot training and certification regulations. In Canada, Transport Canada is responsible for all nautical, rail, road, and aeronautical transportation. Transport Canada sets the standards for examinations and issuing private and commercial pilot licenses.

Some licenses are recognized internationally, while others require additional certifications to be valid in different jurisdictions. A pilot license allows you to fly to another country. However, if you wish to apply for work in another jurisdiction, you must comply with the formalities of transferring the pilot license to that jurisdiction.

Funding Your Pilot Training. Saving up and paying for training out-of-pocket. Aviation schools and organizations may offer financial assistance to deserving candidates. Some banks and institutions provide specialized loans for aviation training.

Addressing The Gender Imbalance in The Pilot Workforce

The pilot workforce is mainly male dominated, often the family's primary income earners. 94 percent of pilots are male, while 6 percent are female. At the same time, Canadian air carriers do not expressly prefer to hire male pilots. Often, males are encouraged to pursue S.T.E.M. (Science, Technology, Engineering, and Math)-related careers. Passengers also perceive a captain to be a male. This gender stereotype can be overcome by including female pilots in onboard safety demonstrations, airline career promotional material, and celebrating the accomplishments of women in aviation once a year. Both genders can equally accomplish the pilot job; therefore, Canada may need to recruit young females into this field.

How Do Female Pilots Perform in The Role of Pilot?

Marie-Line Germain, an internationally recognized scholar and a professor of Human Resources and Leadership states in her research paper that 269 female pilots participated in the pilot training project. Germain says that results show that the lack of acceptance, self-efficacy, social support from organizations, flight instructors, and family, and stereotyping are among the top obstacles women encounter during their flight training, often leading them to quit. Implications for human resource development and women's recruitment, retention, and success in male-dominated occupations.

How Have Other Airlines Addressed the Gender Imbalance In The Pilot Workforce?

This strategy may work for Emirates, which has made significant strides in recruiting female pilots. They have made tremendous progress in creating attractive videos to recruit females into cockpit roles, but more effort needs to be made to include functions outside the cockpit. David Seligson who wrote extensively about women in aviation states that young girls are often not encouraged, or are even discouraged, from making civil aviation a career choice based on mistaken assumptions that many of the jobs involved are not for women or because of preconceptions that girls would not be interested in such employment. Many women do not choose to become pilots due to concerns about pregnancy and family duties, which prevent them from pursuing a career as a pilot.

What Skills and Traits Must A New Pilot Need To Succeed?

A career as a pilot demands a combination of technical skills, mental attributes, and personal characteristics. Here are some qualities that are generally valued. Pilots must have strong cognitive abilities, including problem-solving skills, critical thinking, and the ability to make quick decisions in high-pressure situations. The aviation industry can be stressful, especially during emergencies or challenging weather conditions. Pilots need to manage stress effectively and remain focused on their tasks. New pilots must pay close attention to details during pre-flight checks and while operating the aircraft. This is crucial for safety and the smooth execution of flight plans. Effective communication is essential for pilots, who must interact with air traffic control, cabin crew, and other team members. Clear and concise communication helps prevent misunderstandings and ensures safe operations. Pilots often work in a team with other crew members. Collaborating, sharing responsibilities, and communicating effectively within the cockpit are vital for safe and efficient flight operations. The environment within aviation is dynamic and constantly changing. Pilots must adapt to changing circumstances, such as weather conditions, air traffic, and mechanical issues. Flexibility and the ability to think on one's feet are crucial. Pilots need emotional stability to handle the responsibilities of the job. This includes dealing with long hours, time away from home, and the ability to stay calm under pressure. Pilots must adhere to strict regulations and follow standard operating procedures. Discipline and a sense of responsibility are essential for the safety of the flight and all onboard. While not a psychological trait, good physical health is a prerequisite for pilots. Aviation authorities often have specific medical requirements that pilots must meet to ensure they can handle the physical demands of flying. A genuine passion for flying and a strong desire to pursue a career in aviation can drive success. This passion often translates into dedication and a willingness to improve skills and knowledge continually.

It is important to note that these qualities are generalizations, and individual preferences and requirements may vary among airlines and specific aviation roles.

Flight Training

Canada has several flight training schools and academies where individuals can start pilot training programs. The specific location you choose may depend on factors such as your preferences, budget, and the type of training you are seeking (private pilot license, commercial pilot license, etc.) Flight schools are available across Canada, each offering expertise on flying, including terrain and access to local aviation contacts. When choosing a flight training program, consider factors such as the school's reputation, the instructors' qualifications, the types of aircraft available for training, and any additional resources or support services offered. Additionally, ensure that the school is accredited by the relevant aviation authority in Canada, such as Transport Canada.

Another top training school is located in Daytona Beach, Florida, and Prescott, Arizona: Embry-Riddle Aeronautical University is synonymous with aviation excellence. Known for its comprehensive programs in aviation, aerospace, and engineering, the university offers state-of-the-art facilities and a fleet of over 90 aircraft. Students here not only learn to fly but also gain a deep understanding of the science behind aviation.

Flight Safety Academy in Vero Beach, Florida is also well-known for producing skilled and safe pilots. Focusing on both commercial and private flight training, the academy offers customized programs and boasts an impressive fleet of modern aircraft and simulators.

Chapter 8:
Air Traffic Control

The need for air traffic control is also significant. The aviation industry realized they needed air traffic control for updated weather information, navigation information, and awareness of other aircraft in the area.

In 1903, the Wright Brothers claimed the first flight, which captured the imagination of thousands, but aeronautics lacked the infrastructure needed to operate safely. Their dedication to success led to the discovery of the fundamentals of flight theory and the further development of aviation.

In 1920, the Transcontinental airmail service was established, providing the first airmail service. However, this operation was limited to the daytime, and the main operation would be handed over to the rail service at night. Remember, in those days, pilots relayed on visual flight rules by observing landmarks such as rivers or railroads.

On February 22, 1921, the U.S. postal service started transporting mail between San Francisco and New York at night. One flight would depart the west coast and fly east, while another would depart the east coast and fly west. The story ended in tragedy when the eastbound pilot crashed and died shortly after taking off. The flight leaving New York also crashed when the pilot flew straight into a snowstorm. The pilot survived, but only through the heroism of others who helped him escape death. The early aviation industry is marked by a history of tombstone policies, which have now evolved into safety standard practices.

Moved by compassion and motivation for better flight operations, people established the first aircraft guidance system, a series of rotating lights that dotted the United States. The increase in the speed of aircraft and traffic air density led to concerns about further establishing regulations for air traffic safety. By the 1930s, Cleveland operated the first radio-equipped control room. The early air traffic controllers used maps, mental calculations, and blackboards to ensure safe flight operations within their area.

By the 1950s, the jet age had begun. More people travelled by air over the Atlantic Ocean than by sea, a massive accomplishment for the aviation industry. At the same time, the U.S. Congress passed the Federal Aviation Act of 1958, which would further provide structure and safety to the aviation industry. From 1965 to 1975, the FAA introduced computers to assist with aircraft navigation in the air and on the ground. In 1978, the Airline Deregulation Act dismantled the laws that governed airline pricing and, thus, created a free market for air travel. This intern spurred air travel even further, causing an increase in passenger volume and aircraft movements. By the mid-1990s, computer systems were getting outdated to the point that they caused delays and disruptions to aircraft movements and passengers. Policies were set to create funding for computer upgrades for air traffic control across the United States.

Air Traffic Control Today

Today, in the United States alone, 15,000 skilled workers provide air traffic control services 24 hours a day at 350 locations nationwide. There are stressful roles in a high-energy environment that control the safe movement of aircraft and are responsible for thousands of lives.

During any given hour in the United States, there are about 5,000 aircraft flying over the U.S. airspace at any given time, which is equal to around 50,000 jets a day. How can this operation keep all the aircraft safe at all times?

People may have the misconception that air traffic controllers work exclusively in air traffic control towers. However, Air traffic controllers (A.T.C.s) coordinate the safe movement of aircraft within controlled airspace and on the ground at airports. The system for air traffic control is so vast and complex that it needs to be divided up. The global airspace is divided into nine regions called the International Civil Aviation Organization (I.C.A.O.) and the Global Air Navigation Plan regions.

In the United States and other countries with similar air navigation organization structures, air traffic control is divided into several divisions, including Air Traffic Control System Command Center, Air route traffic control centers, Terminal radar approach control, Air traffic control tower, and Flight service station. As an aircraft flies through a given air space, more than one air traffic controller is responsible for that flight as the plane climbs and descends to different altitudes. Pilots may fly with visual or instrument flight rules depending on the aircraft type. Other air traffic controllers are responsible for different phases of the flight, including pre-flight, take off, departure, on route, descent, approach, and landing.

We can only discuss air traffic control by discussing national sovereignty. This concept touches on a nation and what it includes. Initially, a country was only the surface land where people could walk. However, with air travel, that concept also includes airspace over the land as part of the nation. Therefore, each country has its air traffic control governing authority and rules for who can fly and under which terms. This created the need for air traffic rules to become standardized among nations. Air traffic control is an essential service in Canada and is responsible for the airspace above Canada. However, in the past, when A.T.C. services were on strike, all the aircraft had to fly around the nation due to A.T.C. services not being available. Most countries have their own A.T.C. authority. However, some smaller countries, such as Lichtenstein, have transferred that responsibility to another jurisdiction. Air traffic can be divided into travel speed, altitude levels, geographic areas, and civilian versus military flight operations.

In the United States, A.T.C. services are provided by the F.A.A., the world's busiest airspace. In the United Kingdom, A.T.C. services are supplied by NATS (The National Air Traffic), responsible for 2.5 million flights and 250 passengers annually travelling over the U.K. airspace and the North Atlantic.

In Canada, A.T.C. services are provided by NAV Canada, which is divided into seven areas, each with unique operational characteristics due to terrain, geography, and air traffic flow. Each region is managed by a regional hub known as Area Control Center.

Here is a list of jobs that need A.T.C training or are similar in responsibilities:

- Air traffic controller (A.T.C.)

- Airport air traffic controller
- Enroute air traffic controller
- Flight dispatcher
- Flight service specialist (F.S.S.)
- Instrument flight rules air traffic controller
- Terminal air traffic controller
- Visual flight rules air traffic controller

Where Is The A.T.C Going in The Near Future?

To make significant improvements to how A.T.C operate, the industry needs to face significant challenges head on. The answer is a global ATC tracking system. Just the mention of this, however, is like bringing a herd of wild cats together. Keep in mind that ATC rules and regulations are conducted by each country to protect their sovereign interests. Despite the many challenges, the solution is the ability to track aircraft in real-time, no matter the geographic challenges, such as oceans or terrain.

Cirium integrates Aireon into one global real-time data collection for gate-to-gate aircraft movements. Cirium is the leader in space-based data collection for aircraft. The concept relays on numerous satellites revolving around the globe which rack all modern aircraft equipped with Automatic Dependent Surveillance-Broadcast (ADS-B), anywhere in the world.

Cirium with leading Air Navigation Service Providers (ANSPs) from around the world, including NAV Canada, the Irish Aviation Authority (IAA), Naviair, Enav, NATS (National Air Traffic Services), Eurocontrol and many others. Aireon is the only space-based provider of certified Air Traffic Surveillance (ATS) grade data.

Cirium is receiving transponder signals from ADS-B-equipped aircraft every few seconds across the entire cycle of a flight. This enables the precise positioning of all modern aircraft anywhere in the world. Cirium's data processing team is handling around 1 billion data points every week. Processing the exact location of an aircraft whether they are flying, parked, or stored.

The company states that the most modern aircraft have ADS-B installed. For example, all aircraft that fly in Europe or the U.S. which are heavier than 5.7 tons or that can fly faster than 250 knots must have ADS-B. This includes most commercial passenger and cargo jets and turboprops, such as a Cessna Citation or a Beechcraft 1900 which are both heavier than eight tons. Almost all aircraft have now been fitted with ADS-B transponders. In Europe, 89.4 percent of all registered aircraft and therefore all modern aircraft types, are ADS-B equipped. For the world's major commercial aircraft types, Cirium now has over 99 percent coverage. The company has significantly improved the coverage of unscheduled flights as well, including flights operated using Business Aircraft, Air Taxi and Charter Services, Combi Passenger / Cargo Aircraft, and non-scheduled Passenger and Cargo Aircraft. The game-changing improvements in coverage and detail of flights and aircraft means that Cirium has unsurpassed tracking data worldwide. Not least including extensive coverage in hard-to-track oceanic, mountainous, and remote regions.

"With the integration of Aireon data, Cirium can now track every phase of a flight from pushback to gate arrival and collect every single detail."

This is indeed a game changer for the industry, but will increase aircraft density, efficiency, and will be able to optimize global aircraft movements. This type of progress will also open career opportunities for support staff who can understand the computer programs and interpret the information to further optimize the entire global aircraft operations.

What Does It Take to Become an Air Traffic Controller?

According to Job Bank Canada, the requirement to become an air traffic controller is successful completion of high school. However, a bachelor's degree is recommended, a Bachelor of Aeronautics or an Aviation Degree, but a general Bachelor of Science. It must be 18 years of age and the primary radiotelephone operator's license issued by Transport Canada. Air traffic Controllers and Flight Service Specialists must complete NAV Canada's training program, which includes theoretical and practical exams. Air Traffic Controllers require a license to operate this job function, and flight dispatchers may require a pilot license.

However, the U.S. Bureau of Statistics states that there are several paths to becoming an air traffic controller. Candidates typically need an associate or a bachelor's degree from the Air Traffic Collegiate Training Initiative program, several years of progressively responsible work experience, or a combination of education and experience. They also must be a U.S. citizen, submit to medical and background checks, and complete training at the Federal Aviation Administration (F.A.A.) academy.

In the U.S., the average A.T.C. wage is around $132,000 annually. A.T.C.'s employment outlook is projected to show little or no change from 2022 to 2032. Despite limited employment growth, about 2,000 openings for air traffic controllers are launched each year, on average, over the decade. Most of those openings are expected to result from the need to replace workers who transfer to different occupations or exit the labor force, such as to retire, according to the U.S. Bureau of Statistics, 2023.

While many people apply to become an A.T.C., according to Shmoop, up to 70 percent of the people who apply to become A.T.C. will not be able to complete the training and obtain their license. Because of the strong demand for air travel and upcoming retirement over the next decade, air traffic controllers will enjoy stable job security and progressive career opportunities, even though other employment sectors may show instability. A.T.C. requires the controller to maintain their focus on one area for an extended period, for example, 30 minutes, while the average person's eye drifts away from the point of concentration. A.T.C. are required to stay in good shape during their career, maintain good vision, have a healthy heart and blood pressure, and have no history of mental issues.

A Day in the Life of an A.T.C.

A.T.C. operates 24 hours a day, seven days a week, 365 days a year. Therefore, someone working as an A.T.C. must be flexible and available to cover any shift. Having a supportive pet and family that is very understanding is essential. Getting a good shift depends on seniority and the people you work with. If there are new hires on the change, it increases the stress load for everyone. Typically, A.T.C.s either love their job or hate it. However, the elements that make the job enjoyable are the constantly changing weather conditions, departing or arriving aircraft into your control zone, and sometimes disruptive passengers, which require the aircraft to be delayed.

What is the Career Outlook for A.T.C. in Canada?

According to Canada's Labour Market Outlook, Job Bank Canada projects a labor shortage in the A.T.C. sector until 2031. The workforce's average age is 43, and the retirement age is 62. There are expected 17,100 job openings, while only 11,100 job seekers. The medium wage is around $45.00/hour, requiring a college or apprenticeship program certificate. The tasks involved in this job are the following.

The role of an air traffic controller is both demanding and rewarding, offering a median wage of $45.00 per hour. Candidates looking to enter this field typically require a certificate from a college or an apprenticeship program. The day-to-day tasks of an air traffic controller are diverse and critical for the safety and efficiency of air travel. These responsibilities include authorizing airline flights over assigned routes, directing air traffic within assigned airspace, and providing pilots with vital information for aviation safety. Controllers also co-sign flight authorizations with aircraft captains and manage the movement of both aircraft and service vehicles at airports.

Furthermore, air traffic controllers play a supportive role in overall control operations. They are tasked with checking flight plans for completeness and accuracy, and they have the authority to delay or cancel flights if conditions warrant. Relaying information to pilots in flight, maintaining contact with other control centers, preparing and maintaining various logs and reports, and alerting airport emergency services when necessary are also key aspects of the job.

Controllers must analyze environmental conditions, assess load and fuel capacities, brief flight crews before take-off, and observe, record, and transmit atmospheric and weather information. They also respond to radio calls from aircraft preparing for take-off or landing, providing essential details such as weather conditions, wind speed and direction, and local air traffic.

The ideal candidate for this role must possess a blend of technical and interpersonal skills. Proficiency with technology, computers, and machinery is essential, as is the ability to communicate professionally and with care. Analytical skills, the ability to process information quickly, and coordination with others in a time-sensitive environment are also crucial. Knowledge of communication and transportation laws, public safety, social sciences, and strong mathematical skills round out the profile of a successful air traffic controller candidate.

Job Duties of An Air Traffic Controller

Air traffic controllers play a vital role in ensuring the safety and efficiency of air travel. They are responsible for controlling the flow of air traffic within their assigned airspace, a task they accomplish by using radar monitors, radio, other communication equipment, and visual references. Their duties include issuing take-off and landing instructions to pilots. In addition to these critical tasks, they relay important meteorological, navigational, and other relevant information to pilots during flights.

Another critical aspect of an air traffic controller's role is maintaining consistent radio and telephone contact with adjacent control towers, terminal control units, and other area control centers. This coordination is crucial for managing the smooth movement of aircraft from one area to another. Controllers are also responsible for alerting airport emergency services when aircraft are experiencing difficulties, as well as reporting any missing aircraft to search and rescue services. Moreover, they oversee the activities of all moving aircraft and service vehicles on or near airport runways, ensuring that all operations adhere to strict safety protocols. This comprehensive set of responsibilities underlines the importance of air traffic controllers in maintaining the safety and order of our skies.

Meteorologists

There's another pivotal role that doesn't get as much limelight but are equally as important for the safety and efficiency of air travel—meteorologists. These weather experts play a critical role in the aviation industry, especially at airports, where they analyze and predict weather conditions to ensure safe take-offs and landings.

Meteorologists who deal with aviation forecasts are specialists in their field. Their job goes beyond just predicting rain or sunshine. They analyze complex weather data to provide precise information on wind strength and direction, humidity, visibility, and runway surface conditions. This information is vital for pilots to plan the safest and most efficient flight paths.

One of the most critical factors that meteorologists focus on is wind. Both the strength and direction of wind can significantly impact an aircraft during take-off and landing. Crosswinds, for instance, can make landings challenging and even potentially hazardous. Meteorologists provide real-time data on wind conditions, which is essential for pilots to make informed decisions.

Humidity levels and visibility are other crucial elements in aviation. High humidity can affect engine performance, while low visibility conditions, such as fog, require airports to implement special procedures. Meteorologists help in predicting these conditions, allowing airports to prepare and adjust operations accordingly.

Lastly, when most people think about meteorologists, they don't necessarily think about runways, but meteorologists are also indispensable is in assessing runway surface conditions. Whether it's due to rain, snow, or ice, runways can become slippery, posing significant risks during take-off and landing. Meteorologists play a key role in monitoring these conditions and advising on the necessary safety measures.

Flight Service Specialists

Flight service specialists play a crucial role in aviation safety and efficiency by providing a range of essential services to pilots. Their primary responsibility is to offer pre-flight information, which includes current and forecast weather conditions, radio frequencies, terrain details, airport specifications, and other relevant data. This information is critical for pilots in preparing their flight plans, ensuring they have a comprehensive understanding of the conditions they will encounter.

In addition to disseminating information, flight service specialists are responsible for reviewing flight plans submitted by pilots. They check these plans for completeness and accuracy, a process that is vital for the safety of the flight. Once verified, these plans are then forwarded to the air traffic services facility for further action.

Another key duty of flight service specialists is responding to radio calls from aircraft that are preparing for take-off or landing. In these communications, they provide crucial information such as current weather conditions, wind speed and direction, and the presence of local air traffic. This information helps pilots make informed decisions about their flight operations.

Flight service specialists also support air traffic control operations. They relay radio requests for flight clearances, as well as arrival and departure information and position reports. This role is essential in maintaining the smooth flow of air traffic and ensuring effective communication between pilots and air traffic controllers.

In addition, these specialists are tasked with alerting airport emergency services in case an aircraft experiences difficulties. They also initiate communication searches for aircraft that become overdue, a critical function in ensuring the safety of both the aircraft and its passengers.

Finally, flight service specialists are responsible for observing, recording, and reporting weather conditions at airports. This involves continuous monitoring of environmental factors that could affect flight safety. By fulfilling these various roles, flight service specialists ensure that pilots have the necessary support and information for safe and efficient flight operations.

Flight Dispatchers

In the intricate process of ensuring a safe and efficient flight, various critical steps are undertaken. Initially, there is a thorough analysis of environmental conditions. Specialists assess the aircraft in terms of its load, fuel capacity, and other pivotal factors. This assessment is crucial to determine the most suitable flight routes, ensuring both safety and efficiency. Following this, the flight crew is briefed before take-off. This briefing encompasses a range of important information including current weather conditions and the status of maritime facilities and airports along the route. Such briefings are essential for the crew to be fully prepared for any eventualities during the flight.

Another important step in this process is the co-signing of flight authorization. This is typically done in conjunction with the aircraft captain, symbolizing a mutual agreement and understanding of the flight's readiness. Throughout the flight's duration, there is continuous monitoring of its progress. Communication with the aircraft is maintained as required, enabling real-time updates and support as the flight proceeds.

Under certain circumstances, flights may need to be delayed or even cancelled if conditions warrant such action. This decision is made with the utmost consideration for the safety of passengers and crew. Lastly, there is a meticulous task of preparing and maintaining flight plans, flight logs, and other related reports. These documents are not only vital for the current flight but also serve as important records for future reference and analysis. Each of these steps plays a vital role in the overarching goal of ensuring a safe, efficient, and a well-coordinated flight.

Chapter 9:
Venturing Into Aircraft Engineering

So, if you are reading this chapter, then you are interested in becoming an aircraft engineer. But before you invest in various diplomas and certificates, it is wise to consider what it takes to become successful in this career field.

A Walk Around the Hangar at Air Canada.

In the late 90s, I had just joined Air Canada, and as part of our flight attendant program, we visited the Air Canada hangar at the Vancouver International Airport. I was late for my class, and rushed to where I thought I was supposed to go. In a panic, I passed through these double swing doors and innocently wandered down a hallway. Realizing that I was lost, and feeling even more panicked that I was missing the tour, I walked through a second door and found myself in an enormous hangar. To my surprise, the gigantic Boeing 747 was parked in front of me. Her massive wings spanned the entire hangar, almost touching the sides. I was gobsmacked by her towering beauty, her elegant body, her arching nose, and her powerful engines, all cast shows on the hangar floor. To fly inside was truly a privilege, but to walk up close to the Queen of Sky was truly a once-in-a-lifetime experience. Various aircraft maintenance equipment filled the hangar.

I just stared, not moving. Nobody questioned me. Nobody asked what I was doing. Of course, this was before 9/11. Nowadays, you can't get close to any commercial airplane without some sort of security check. I'm thankful because it was at that time, that I truly realized the significance and the massive operation aircraft maintenance really is. Since that day, I have a deep respect for the men and women who dedicate their lives to the maintenance of aircraft and their safety.

Aircraft Maintenance and Aircraft Engineering Careers.

Aircraft maintenance and engineering encompass a range of aviation roles that make a significant contribution to the safety and efficient operation of the aviation industry. This large occupational group can be divided into these areas:

- Aircraft Maintenance Technician
- Avionics Technician
- Aircraft Inspector
- Aerospace Engineer
- Structural Engineer
- Quality Assurance Specialist,
- Technical Writer
- Logistics And Parts Supply Manager,
- Aviation Safety Manager
- Aircraft Hangar Project Manager
- Aircraft gas turbine engine technician
- Aircraft Hydraulics Mechanic
- Aircraft Inspector
- Aircraft Maintenance Engineer (Ame) (Except Avionics)
- Aircraft Mechanic
- Aircraft Repair And Overhaul Inspector
- Aircraft Repair Shop Inspector
- Aircraft Structural Repair Technician
- Aircraft Systems Inspector
- Aviation Mechanical Component Shop Technician
- Certified Aircraft Technician
- Flight Test Inspector

As a team, these occupations work together to ensure the safety, reliability and efficiency that has become the hallmark of the aviation industry. The variations of the job functions of these roles depends on the size of the organization, the scope of responsibility, and the type of aircraft which feature different engine types, including single-engine, turboprop, jet engine, or rotary engines.

Which Career Direction Is Right For You?

Choosing which career direction within the above-mentioned roles will depend on your personal interests and skill set, the occupational research, and the requirements for that role within your geographic area or desired work territory, the access to education and training, your networking skills, and finally your career goals and industry trends.

Historically, an aircraft engineer or mechanic was perceived similar as an automobile mechanic, a guy working in hangar taking greasy engines apart and looking for spare parts. However, the industry has evolved significantly since those days. Now, the occupation of aircraft mechanic is high-tech, involving robotics assembly, computer analytics, avionics, and navigational aids. Together they form a various occupational groups including aircraft mechanic, aircraft design engineers, propulsion engineers, and composite engineering specialists, aerospace mechanical engineers, and avionics and navigational engineers just to name a few. In this chapter we will take a closer look at some of the occupations that make this occupational group.

What Is an Aircraft Mechanic and What Do They Do?

An aircraft mechanic, also known as an aircraft maintenance technician, services and repairs various aircraft parts and prepares the aircraft to be put back into operational service. They control numerous moving parts of an aircraft, including single engine, jet engine, and helicopter aircraft. Commercial airlines, private aircraft owns as well as the military seek the skills of an aircraft mechanic to make the aircraft serviceable. Aircraft are also very complex machines and have many moving parts as well as instruments that enable the aircraft to safely fly from point of origin and its destination. Unlike a vehicle that can pull over when there is a mechanical problem, once up in the air, it is more difficult because the pilot is required to land the aircraft safety before the issue can be addressed.

Aircraft mechanics conduct audits of an aircraft, identify the broken part, and replace it with a new part, repair, test and document the repair process in the maintenance logbook.

The keys skills to become an aircraft mechanic are troubleshooting, creativity, communication, and collaboration. When the aircraft is on scheduled maintenance the time is allocated, however, sometimes the work must be completed as the pilot crew and passengers are waiting for a solution, which adds the more time pressure to complete the given task.

What Is an Avionics Engineer and What Do They Do?

An avionics engineer is a critical part of today's aeronautical workforce that enable aircraft to fly the distances. They are responsible for the electrical and navigational components of an aircraft.

The original aircraft were designed with cables and pullies. Pilots pulling on the controls literally moved the aircraft part with cables. Now, these systems have been replaced by computers and electrical systems which an avionics engineer is responsible for. In addition, avionics engineers are also responsible for the efficient operation of satellite systems, including the communication systems, navigation systems, and display systems on board aircraft of all types.

Most aircraft engineers have a bachelor's degree in avionics studies from a college or university, which may offer a coop program to transition from the academic environment to the workplace environment. Often, avionics degree courses include general engineering principles, structures, mechanics, aerodynamics, and electronics.

The wags for an avionics engineer vary but range between $38,000 to $100,000 depending on experience, the scope of work, and the employer.

What Skills Do You Need for Avionics?

As an aviation technician, the interpretation of design plays a pivotal role. It's not just about understanding the complex electronic and aviation designs; it's about bringing them to life in the real world. For an avionics technician, being adept at this means being able to work effectively with intricate aircraft systems. It's this skill that bridges the gap between theoretical designs and practical application, ensuring that the implementation of design specifications and modifications is as accurate as possible. This accuracy is critical as it ensures that aircraft systems function precisely as intended, a non-negotiable in the field of aviation where safety is paramount.

The Criticality of Attention to Detail

Attention to detail is more than a skill in avionics; it's a necessity. In an environment where a small oversight can lead to significant consequences, the ability to notice even the most minute details becomes crucial. This high level of precision in tasks leads to safer and more reliable aircraft operations. For an avionics technician, having a keen eye for detail means ensuring that every component and system operates flawlessly, contributing to the overall safety and reliability of the aircraft.

The Power of Collaborative Working

Avionics is not a solo journey. It's a field where teamwork is essential, and collaborative working becomes a key skill. Technicians often find themselves in group settings, working alongside engineers, pilots, and other technicians. This collaborative effort is not just about getting along with others but also about promoting effective communication and coordination. It's through this synergy that complex aircraft systems are maintained efficiently, ensuring operational excellence and safety.

Reporting and Communication

The importance of clear communication and accurate reporting cannot be overstated. These skills are vital for documenting maintenance procedures and conveying technical information. They ensure that all vital information is not just recorded, but also shared accurately and consistently among team members and other stakeholders. This uniform understanding is crucial in maintaining a smooth and error-free operation within the highly technical and precise field of avionics.

Problem-Solving and Diagnostic Skills

Facing and solving complex problems quickly and efficiently is at the heart of an avionics technician's role. These skills become indispensable, especially when dealing with sophisticated aircraft electronics. They enhance a technician's capability to diagnose issues promptly and rectify them, which is essential in reducing downtime and enhancing safety. This quick problem-solving ability ensures that aircraft remain operational and safe, a testament to the technician's expertise and skill.

The Need for Methodical Working

Avionics is a field that demands a systematic and methodical approach to tasks. This systematic approach ensures thoroughness and accuracy in every task undertaken. It leads to more organized and efficient work processes, which are critical in minimizing errors and enhancing the overall performance of the aircraft's electronic systems. For an avionics technician, being methodical is not just a way of working; it's a way of ensuring excellence and reliability in every aspect of their job.

Equipment Maintenance

Regular maintenance and upkeep of avionics equipment are essential for its optimal operation. This routine care ensures the longevity and reliability of the aircraft's electronic systems, directly impacting operational safety. For avionics technicians, this ongoing maintenance work is a critical component of their role, ensuring that every piece of equipment operates at its best, every time.

Mathematical Skills in Avionics

In avionics, strong mathematical skills are more than just an academic requirement; they are a practical necessity. These skills are required for a range of calculations and analyses. They support accurate measurements, calculations, and conversions, all of which are fundamental in the technical tasks and the decision-making processes in avionics. For technicians, being proficient in mathematics means being able to handle the quantitative aspects of their job with ease and accuracy, ensuring that every calculation contributes to the safe and effective operation of the aircraft.

What is an Aircraft Inspector?

An aircraft inspector is a professional tasked with inspecting aircraft and aircraft systems. This role is critical following the manufacture, modification, maintenance, repair, or overhaul of aircraft. These inspectors are employed across various sectors in the aviation industry, including aircraft manufacturing, maintenance, repair, and overhaul establishments, as well as airlines and other aircraft operators. Additionally, apprentices in this field are also considered part of this unit group, learning the ropes under the guidance of experienced inspectors.

The Responsibilities of an Aircraft Inspector

Inspection of Structural and Mechanical Systems: Aircraft inspectors are responsible for examining the structural and mechanical systems of aircraft. Their primary focus is to ensure that these systems meet the stringent standards set by government regulations and the operating company. This aspect of their job is crucial in ascertaining the overall performance and safety of the aircraft.

Ensuring Compliance with Standards: An important part of their job is to inspect the work done by aircraft mechanics. This includes maintenance, repair, overhaul, or modification of aircraft and their mechanical systems. The inspectors ensure that these tasks are carried out according to established standards and procedures, maintaining the high quality and safety standards of the aviation industry.

Record Maintenance: Maintaining detailed repair, inspection, and certification records of aircraft is another key responsibility. These records are essential for tracking the history of the aircraft, ensuring compliance with safety regulations, and providing valuable data for future inspections and maintenance work.

The Importance of Aircraft Inspectors

Aircraft Inspectors play a pivotal role in the aviation industry. Their expertise and vigilance ensure that every aircraft that takes to the skies is safe and airworthy. Essentially, they act as the guardians of aviation safety, ensuring that every component of an aircraft, whether it's a tiny bolt or a complex engine system, is in top condition. Their work not only ensures the safety of the passengers and crew but also contributes to the overall trust in air travel.

The wages for an aircraft inspector range from $22 to $49/hr, however there may be variations of this wage from province to province based on local supply and demand and the relative cost of living. The demand for aircraft inspectors also varies from province to province with the highest demand in Ontario.

What Does an Aerospace Engineer Do?

Aerospace engineering is a field that combines creativity and precision to push the boundaries of what's possible in air and space travel. Aerospace engineers are the driving force behind the design, development, and innovation of aircraft, spacecraft, and beyond. Aerospace engineers research, design and develop aerospace vehicles, aerospace systems and their components, and perform duties related to their testing, evaluation, installation, operation, and maintenance. They are employed by aircraft and spacecraft manufacturers, air transport carriers, and in government and educational and research institutions.

Job Duties of an Aerospace Engineer

Aerospace engineers are at the forefront of designing and developing aerospace vehicles and systems. This includes a vast range of technologies such as aircraft, spacecraft, missiles, satellites, and even space-based communication systems. Their work involves not just conceptualizing these vehicles but also bringing them to life through meticulous design and development processes.

A critical aspect of their work involves conducting computer simulations of aerospace vehicles, systems, and components. Utilizing advanced mathematical modelling, these simulations allow engineers to test and refine designs, ensuring functionality and safety before they are physically built.

Aerospace engineers also prepare specifications for the materials and processes used in aerospace manufacturing, maintenance, repair, or modification. This task is crucial in ensuring that every component used in aerospace vehicles meets the required standards of durability, safety, and performance.

The role often involves supervising and coordinating the manufacturing, assembly, modification, repair, and overhaul of aircraft and spacecraft. This managerial aspect ensures that every phase of the construction and maintenance process aligns with the project's specifications and quality standards.

Coordinating ground and flight tests of air and spacecraft is another vital responsibility. This process is essential for validating the design and functionality of aerospace vehicles under various conditions, ensuring they are ready for real-world operation.

Operational and Maintenance Guidelines

Developing operational specifications, maintenance schedules, and manuals for operators is an integral part of their job. This ensures that those who operate or maintain aerospace vehicles have clear, comprehensive guidelines, enhancing safety and efficiency.

Logistical and Operational Support

Aerospace engineers are involved in developing the technical phases of logistical and operational support for aerospace vehicles and systems. Their expertise is crucial in ensuring that these complex machines receive the necessary support throughout their lifecycle.

Investigation and Reporting

In the event of structural failures, accidents, or incidents, aerospace engineers investigate and report on these occurrences. They prepare recommendations for corrective action, playing a critical role in preventing future mishaps and enhancing the safety of aerospace vehicles and systems.

What Does a Structural Engineer Do, And How Do You Become One?

In the field of aerospace engineering, the role of a structural engineer is multifaceted and critical to the overall success of any aerospace project. An aerospace structural engineer is responsible for researching, analyzing, and creating structural engineering specifications.

Utilizing advanced computer software, aerospace structural engineers meticulously craft and modify prototypes. These prototypes are more than just preliminary models; they are integral in predicting and understanding how various structures will perform under a myriad of conditions. This aspect of their work is not just about creating; it's about foreseeing and ensuring that every design aspect is optimized for the real-world challenges it will face.

Central to the role of an aerospace structural engineer is the assurance of structural integrity. This aspect of their work is all about strength and resilience. The engineers focus intently on ensuring that the physical structure of aerospace vehicles – be it an airplane or a spacecraft – is robust enough to withstand the stresses of operation. This includes everything from the rigors of take-off to the challenges of flight, and the critical moments of landing. Their expertise ensures that these complex vehicles are not just designed for performance but also for enduring safety and reliability.

Collaboration is another cornerstone of their role. Like everybody in the aviation industry, aerospace structural engineers do not work in isolation; they must embody teamwork in order to get the job done. For starters, they work closely with other engineers and various teams, contributing their specialized knowledge to the broader design and functionality of aerospace vehicles. This collaborative effort is vital in bringing together different perspectives and expertise, ensuring the holistic success of the project. Through their combined efforts, the team ensures that every aspect of the aerospace vehicle is finely tuned and harmoniously integrated for optimal performance.

What Is The Career Path For A Quality Assurance Specialist?

The notion of quality assurance (or QA) implies that the same quality standards are achieved by different people performing the same job function. This is very important for organizations that have shift work so ensuring strong communication and oversight is key. An Aviation Quality Assurance Specialist makes sure that the same work quality standards are attained across the organization.

The typical career path for a quality assurance specialist starts with an entry-level position as a software tester or quality assurance technician. As you gain experience in this position, you can move up to more senior roles, such as quality assurance analyst, quality assurance engineer, or quality assurance manager.

"Quality assurance has been in the corporate world and industry for many years. It is indicative of excellence and compliance with standards. In simple terms, Quality is the standard of something as measured against other things of a similar kind, the degree of excellence or an improvement in product quality. It is brought about by strict and consistent commitment to certain standards that achieve uniformity of a product to satisfy specific customer or user requirements. For example, in manufacturing, it is a measure of excellence or a state of being free from defects, deficiencies, and significant variations. Quality assurance focuses on planning, approach, techniques, and processes. It is working as a managing tool to prevent defects. It is proactive and preventative in nature. According to ISO definition, it states that quality assurance is all those planned and systematic actions necessary to provide adequate confidence that an entity will fulfill requirements for quality. Both the customers and the managers have a need for quality assurance as they cannot oversee operations for themselves. Quality assurance can be the sum of all actions taken to provide assurance that the desired outputs will be attained. Quality assurance considers all aspects of a process, from planning to completion, and identifies weak points that could be prone to the introduction of errors. In essence, quality assurance is determining the gaps based on non-compliance with either the regulatory requirements or organizational requirements. The primary purpose of the QA System is not to find defects, rather confirming the satisfactory operation of the system. The quality assurance audits are done by QA auditors." (Aviationhunt Team, 2023)

Aircraft Logistics and Parts Supply Manager

This is a very important part of aircraft maintenance. The wrong part installed on an aircraft could cause that aircraft to have trouble at 35,000 feet in the air. On 10 June 1990, the BAC 111 528FL suffered an explosive decompression. While the aircraft was flying over Didcot,

Oxfordshire, an improperly installed windscreen panel separated from its frame, causing the captain to be partially ejected from the aircraft.

"According to a report by the Air Accidents Investigation Branch, a fitter had used the wrong bolts to secure the windscreen 27 hours before the flight. The report said the process was characterised by a series of poor work practices, poor judgements, and perceptual errors. The bizarre drama was recreated for a documentary called Air Crash Investigation - Blow Out, which was aired on the National Geographic Channel in 2005."

This incident reinforces the importance of a qualified parts supply manager who follows specific aircraft maintenance policies.

Aircraft Hangar Project Manager

An Aircraft Hangar Project Manager holds an important role that requires reporting directly to the Senior Project Manager. This position involves a multifaceted approach to aviation-related projects, primarily focusing on general aviation and commercial air service airports. The core responsibilities encompass a broad spectrum of tasks, including aviation civil design, planning, construction support, and client management.

When it comes to civil design and engineering, the Project Manager is tasked with designing aircraft hangars and associated facilities. This generally includes careful consideration of various factors such as size, materials, and environmental impact. They are also responsible for performing engineering tasks that involve structural analysis, load calculations, and ensuring compliance with aviation standards.

Institution	Aerospace / Aeronautical Engineering	Aircraft Maintenance	Aircraft Structural Repair	Avionics Maintenance	Business Administration	Chemical Engineering	Electrical Engineering	Electronics Engineering	Industrial Design	Manufacturing / Industrial Engineering	Materials Engineering	Mechanical Engineering	Mechatronics Engineering	Nanotechnology Engineering	Quality Engineering	Software Engineering	Space Engineering	Systems Engineering
Canadore College		T	T	T	T							T						
Carleton University	BMD				BM		BMD	BM			M	BMD				B		BMD
Centennial College		T		T	T						T	T						
Fanshawe College School of Aviation Technology		T	T	T														
McMaster Manufacturing Research Institute (MMRI) - McMaster University										MD		MD						
Mohawk College		T	T												T			
Ryerson University, Department of Aerospace Engineering	BMD																	BMD
University of Ontario Institute of Technology					M		BMD	B				BMD						
University of Ottawa						BMD				MD		BMD						
University of Toronto, Institute for Multidisciplinary Design and Innovation (UT-IMDI)	BMD						BMD			BMD		BMD					BMD	
University of Waterloo					BMD	BMD	BMD					BMD	BMD	B				BMD
University of Windsor				BM			BMD			BMD		BMD						

Legend: T Technician B Bachelor Degree M Master's Degree D Doctorate (PhD)

Chapter 10:
Aviation Management

During my employment with Air Transat, one of the things that I appreciated most was that our executive team would make a tour of all the bases and meet with the front-line workers and staff twice a year. Flight attendants were also invited to attend a meeting which lasted the whole afternoon. The C.E.O. at the time made the trip across the country as well. During the presentation, a review of the previous season was discussed, such as total passengers flown on our network, the increase in the number of flights, and destinations, the cost of fuel, and any prospecting of new routes or joint ventures.

At the end of the meeting, an invitation was extended that if anybody wanted to meet with the CEO, they could and that he had an open-door policy. Well, a few years later, I was in Montreal, and I wanted to take him up on his invitation. I made my way to the new head office, with ceilings that were 5 stories high, and took the elevator to the executive floor. The receptionist welcomed me as a crew member and called the CEO and VP of Inflight Services. To my surprise, within 30 minutes, both came to attend to my enquiry and the reason for my visit.

It was at this point that I realized the power of strong leadership and eliminating inefficiencies within an organization. The executive office with made of glass, representing transparency in communication within the company. The executive team implemented new strategies to increase revenues which included a full buy on board menu, scales on both outbound and inbound check-in resulting in added revenue to the company, optimized flight schedules and crew management to make layovers more efficient and cost effective. The goal of an airline CEO is, of course, to maximize profits for the shareholders while giving the customer / the passenger what they want. At the end of the day, the passengers want to get to their destination with their bags on time. Understanding this strong motivator, the CEO did everything possible to remove barriers which were the root causes for delayed flights and increased positive passenger – luggage matches. He also addressed deficiencies found on the aircraft. While the aircraft was on the ground, a designated crew went on board fixing broken lights, TV screens, reclinable seats, etc. over a period of 6 months, aircraft were operating with zero snags, enhancing the passenger travel experience. Seeing this transformation inspired me to study aviation management as a career path.

Choosing a career as Aviation Manager, opens many opportunities to have a positive impact on the aviation industry in airport management roles, airline management roles, as well as government roles. This career choice also requires a bit of planning and strategy. Ideally, the candidate would start with an undergraduate degree business-related background such as business administration, business law, International Business Administration, Sales and Marketing degrees, with an emphasis on computer programs. Once positioned in the organization of your choice, then proceed with the master's studies in aviation management, such as offered by Griffith University or Embrey Riddle University, with a focus on an aspect of aviation that will enhance your career.

Some of the career opportunities include the following:

- Airport Manager
- Airline Manager
- Aviation Operations Manager
- Aviation Safety Manger
- Airport Security Manager
- Aviation Finance Manager
- Aviation Sales and Marketing Manager
- Airline Fleet Manager
- Training and Operational Standards Manager
- Airline or Airport Customer Experience Manager

Airport Manager/Director

This position is pivotal in ensuring the smooth and efficient functioning of an airport. The responsibilities of an Airport Manager/Director are comprehensive, encompassing the oversight of various critical aspects of airport operations.

At the heart of their role lies the management of the airport terminal, a complex task that involves coordinating numerous activities to ensure passenger comfort and efficient terminal operations. This includes everything from the management of check-in counters to the smooth handling of baggage systems and the provision of amenities and services that enhance the traveller's experience.

Security is another critical area under the purview of the Airport Manager/Director. Ensuring the safety and security of passengers, staff, and the entire airport facility is paramount. This involves overseeing stringent security measures, implementing, and updating security protocols, and ensuring compliance with national and international security regulations.

Airfield maintenance is also a significant part of their responsibilities. The Airport Manager/Director oversees the maintenance of runways, taxiways, and the surrounding airfield. This not only involves regular maintenance to ensure safety and efficiency, but also planning and overseeing any necessary upgrades or expansions to meet the evolving needs of the airport.

Strong organizational skills are essential, as the role requires the coordination of multiple departments and activities. Leadership skills are equally important, as this role involves guiding and motivating a wide range of teams, from security personnel to maintenance staff. A deep knowledge of aviation regulations is also crucial, ensuring that the airport operates within the legal framework set by aviation authorities.

The responsibilities of an airport or airline operations manager also extend to the broader aspect of facility operation management. This involves planning, organizing, directing, controlling, and evaluating the operations of facilities that may include not just the airport but also associated real estate such as shopping centers, convention centers, and recreational areas within the airport complex.

Employed by a diverse range of establishments, the Airport Manager/Director plays a crucial role in ensuring that everything operates smoothly and efficiently, whether it's a commercial, transportation, or recreational facility.

What is the Role of The Facility Operation Manager?

Facility Operation Managers are tasked with the comprehensive oversight of commercial, transportation, and recreational facilities, along with the real estate they encompass. Their duties encompass the strategic planning, organization, direction, control, and evaluation of these facilities. One of their primary responsibilities includes overseeing the leasing of space, not just within the facility but also everything that is included as part of the real estate. This extends to the development and implementation of effective marketing strategies to maximize occupancy and use.

In addition to space management, Facility Operation Managers are responsible for the coordination of a range of administrative services. These services cover a broad range of areas, including signage, cleaning, maintenance, parking, safety inspections, security measures, and even snow removal. Each of these areas requires a detailed and organized approach to ensure the facility operates smoothly and meets the needs of its occupants and visitors.

These managers might also be partly responsible for some construction projects. These responsible can include planning, organizing, directing, controlling, and evaluating construction endeavors aimed at modifying the existing facilities. This role demands a keen eye for detail and a strong sense of project management to ensure that modifications meet the required standards and objectives.

Another crucial aspect of their job is overseeing the installation, maintenance, and repair of the facility's infrastructure. This includes a wide range of systems, from machinery and equipment to electrical and mechanical systems, ensuring that every aspect of the facility's infrastructure is functioning optimally.

Facility Operation Managers are also tasked with planning and managing the facility's operational budget, balancing costs with the need for quality services and infrastructure. Additionally, they are responsible for preparing or overseeing the preparation of reports and statistics that provide insights into various areas of their responsibility.

Another significant part of their role involves human resources management for anything facility related. They hire staff, oversee their training, and supervise their work, ensuring that the team is skilled, efficient, and well-coordinated.

Maintenance Managers share some similarities with Facility Operation Managers, particularly in their focus on the maintenance and repair of an establishment's machinery, equipment, and electrical and mechanical systems. Their role is crucial in ensuring that all operational equipment is in top condition, preventing breakdowns and disruptions in the facility's daily activities.

They develop and implement schedules and procedures for regular safety inspections and preventive maintenance programs. This proactive approach is vital in maintaining the safety and functionality of the facility.

Maintenance Managers also coordinate essential services like cleaning, snow removal, and landscaping. They ensure that these operations are carried out efficiently and effectively, maintaining the aesthetic and functional integrity of the facility.

Contract administration is another aspect of their role. They administer contracts for the provision of supplies and services, ensuring that these contracts meet the facility's needs both in terms of quality and cost-effectiveness.

Like their counterparts in facility operations, Maintenance Managers are also involved in human resources management. They hire staff and oversee their training and supervision, building a team that is competent and capable of maintaining the facility to the highest standards.

Wages for an Airport Operations Manager varies from $24.84 to $67.31 which is equal to around $48,000 to $134,000 annually. However, the range may not be the same for all airport across North America which varies with the local cost of living, the size of the operation and the level of experience of the person. The average age of this occupational group is 48 years old, and the age of retirement is 65 years old. This occupational group will see 11,100 job openings, while the new candidates are around 9,500, according to Job Bank Canada.

Airline Manager

An Airline Manager is responsible for overseeing various aspects of airline operations. This includes managing tasks like scheduling flights, budgeting, and ensuring the airline complies with all safety and regulatory standards. Essential skills for this role include strong business acumen to make informed financial decisions, strategic planning abilities to optimize operations and foresee industry trends, and effective communication skills to liaise with different departments, stakeholders, and regulatory bodies. These competencies are crucial in ensuring the smooth and profitable running of airline operations.

During my career and the last 20 years of professional life experience, the book that inspired me the most, which related to airline management, was 'From Worst to First' by Gordon Bethune. In his book, he describes the amazing process of how he turned Continental Airlines from the worst airline to fly on to the best airline in the 1990s. One concept that he really drove home in his book was you can make a pizza so cheap that nobody wants to eat it. With an airline, the same business model rings too. The CEO of Continental incorporated the concept that if you want to improve a component or aspect of the business, one must start to track it. The company was losing $5 million per month, due to poor on-time performance. They started tracking on-time performance, positive passenger / luggage matches, inventory, the time to turn around an aircraft, etc. To motivate the staff, he motivated each department to contribute towards on time performance. Within 2 months, the on-time performance was the best in the industry. Passengers want to leave on time and arrive on time, so that they can get to the beach, make the connecting flight, or attend a business meeting. By working together as a team, the airline was able to give the passengers what they wanted AND save money at the same time due to passenger compensation and added operational fees. He also implemented a strategy which would invest in aviation-related education and professional development. One board member asked, "What happens if we invest in people, and then they leave?" The CEO replied, "What if we don't invest in our employees and they stay?" Throughout the book, he gives numerous examples of how this strategy worked. Even today, you can see many airlines incorporate the strategies that Continental Airlines used to turn the airline around from the worst to the best in the industry.

While the book mentions numerous airline improvement models, I don't want to rewrite his book. However, his example has been a role model for me in how I seek to improve my operations and inspire others.

Aviation Operations Manager

The role of an Aviation Operations Manager is dynamic and crucial in the fast-paced world of aviation. Tasked with the responsibility of coordinating and managing the day-to-day operations of aviation services, these professionals are at the heart of ensuring efficient and safe air travel.

In their role, Aviation Operations Managers oversee a range of crucial activities, from ground services and logistics to flight dispatch. This involves a meticulous orchestration of various elements to ensure that all operations run smoothly and according to schedule. Ground services, a critical component of airport operations, involve numerous tasks such as baggage handling, aircraft refuelling, and passenger services. Logistics encompasses the complex coordination of flight schedules, crew management, and the maintenance of aircraft. Flight dispatch is another critical area involving the planning and monitoring of flights, ensuring they adhere to safety regulations and operational protocols.

To excel in this role, an Aviation Operations Manager must possess a set of specialized skills. Strong organizational skills are paramount, as the job requires the ability to manage multiple tasks and coordinate various operations simultaneously. Attention to detail is another essential skill, given the complexity and precision required in aviation operations. The ability to work under pressure is also critical, as the aviation industry is known for its fast-paced and sometimes unpredictable nature.

In recent years, the approach to aviation management has evolved significantly. The modern management philosophy in aviation is an approach that focuses on balancing the needs of the individual with those of the organization as a whole. This contemporary perspective seeks to create an environment where employees are not just instructed but empowered. Empowerment in this context means giving employees the autonomy to make decisions and providing them with the necessary resources and support to achieve their objectives. This philosophy, which gained prominence around February 2023, emphasizes the importance of nurturing a workplace where every member of the team can contribute effectively and feel valued.

This shift in management style is reflective of a broader change in the industry's approach to operations. It signifies a move away from top-down, rigid management structures to more flexible and dynamic models. This new philosophy is about fostering a collaborative environment where innovation and efficiency are encouraged, and where employees are motivated to take initiative and responsibility.

In essence, the role of an Aviation Operations Manager today is not just about managing operations but also about leading people and driving change. It's about creating a work environment that is responsive to the needs of both the employees and the organization, ensuring that the aviation operations are not only efficient and safe but also adaptable and forward-thinking.

Aviation Safety Manager

An Aviation Safety Manager primarily focuses on the development and implementation of safety programs. Their responsibilities extend to conducting thorough risk assessments and ensuring strict compliance with all relevant safety regulations. This role is pivotal in maintaining the highest standards of safety within the aviation sector.

The core duty of an Aviation Safety Manager involves the creation and execution of comprehensive safety programs. These programs are designed to preemptively identify potential safety hazards and implement measures to mitigate any risks associated with aviation operations. This proactive approach is essential in minimizing accidents and ensuring the well-being of both staff and passengers.

Conducting risk assessments is another significant aspect of the role. The Aviation Safety Manager systematically evaluates various operational scenarios to identify any potential risks. This process involves analyzing different facets of aviation operations, from in-flight procedures to ground handling and maintenance activities. By assessing these elements, the Safety Manager can devise strategies to reduce the likelihood of accidents and enhance overall safety.

Ensuring compliance with safety regulations is a continuous responsibility. The Aviation Safety Manager is required to stay abreast of the latest aviation safety regulations and standards. They are responsible for ensuring that all operations within their domain adhere to these regulations, thereby maintaining legal compliance and promoting a safe operating environment.

When it comes to skills, an Aviation Safety Manager must, of course, possess an in-depth knowledge of aviation safety regulations. This expertise is fundamental in understanding the complexities of the aviation industry and implementing effective safety measures. Analytical skills are equally important, as they enable the Safety Manager to dissect various operations and identify underlying risks.

Aviation safety has also evolved a lot. In the early days, if there was an accident, the blame would usually be placed at the person who did not follow SOPs (standard operating procedures).

However, Safety and evolved to setting Safety Management Systems (SMS) in place. There are several different strategies to look at why accidents happen or analyse who is responsible for an accident. It doesn't matter if it is big or small. Typically, there are several or compounding events that lead up to the event, and the responsibility is shared between several parties.

To help with the investigation process, SMS uses a number of root cause analysis methods which include, the Swiss Cheese Method, Bow Tie Method, Fish Bone Method, to name a few. They also gather information using interviews, equipment, drones, to draw conclusions and make recommendations.

ICAO also offers courses about aviation safety trends at all levels that affect security.

You can find more information at this link.
https://www.icao.int/safety/airnavigation/AIG/Pages/Investigative-Technologies-and-Techniques.aspx

Airport Security Manager

The role of an Airport Security Manager is a critical and a demanding one, central to the safe and secure functioning of airports worldwide. As the person in charge of overseeing all security measures and procedures at the airport, this manager plays a pivotal role in ensuring the safety of passengers, staff, and airport facilities.

An Airport Security Manager's responsibilities encompass a broad range of tasks aimed at maintaining a secure environment. This involves the meticulous implementation of security protocols that are designed to protect against a variety of threats. These protocols cover multiple aspects of airport operations, from passenger screening to baggage checks and even the safeguarding of restricted areas. The manager is also responsible for the continual assessment and improvement of these security measures, ensuring they remain effective and are in line with current threats and regulatory requirements.

A critical aspect of this role involves risk management. This includes identifying potential security risks and vulnerabilities within the airport and developing strategies to mitigate these risks. The Airport Security Manager must also have a deep understanding of various security procedures and be adept at anticipating potential security challenges. This foresight is crucial in preventing security breaches and ensuring the safety of all those within the airport.

The ability to respond quickly and effectively to security incidents is an essential skill for an Airport Security Manager. This requires not only a calm and decisive approach in the face of emergencies, but also the ability to coordinate effectively with various agencies, such as law enforcement, emergency services, and airport staff. The manager must lead the response during security incidents, ensuring that appropriate actions are taken swiftly to resolve any issues while minimizing disruption to airport operations and ensuring the safety of all involved.

Furthermore, an Airport Security Manager is often involved in training and supervising security personnel, ensuring they are well-prepared to handle a range of security scenarios. This includes regular drills and exercises to keep the team alert and ready for any eventuality.

In addition to their security-specific responsibilities, Airport Security Managers often play a role in the broader management of the airport. This can include collaborating with other departments to ensure that security measures are integrated smoothly into the overall operation of the airport and do not unnecessarily impede the flow of passengers and goods.

They also deal with mundane security issues such as abandoned suitcases which need to be collected and destroyed, trespassing onto the airport property, traffic flow management, passenger screening, disruptive passengers both on the non-secured side as well as in the restricted areas of the airport, and on the airfield. They also respond to breaches such as vehicles crashing into the airport fence, drones, and can include wildlife management.

Aviation Finance Manager

The Aviation Finance Manager plays a crucial role in the financial health and strategic planning of aviation organizations. This position involves a multifaceted approach to managing the organization's finances, ensuring both short-term functionality and long-term financial stability.

One of the primary responsibilities of an Aviation Finance Manager is the creation and management of budgets and so this person must have a strong financial and mathematical background. This position also requires a detailed understanding of the organization's financial inflows and outflows, as well as the ability to forecast future financial needs. Crafting a budget that aligns with the organization's goals involves not just accounting for current financial realities but also anticipating future challenges and opportunities. This ensures the organization can operate efficiently while also investing in growth and development.

In addition to budgeting, the Aviation Finance Manager is also responsible for financial reporting. This involves the regular preparation of detailed financial statements that provide insights into the organization's financial health. These reports are crucial for stakeholders, including management, investors, and regulatory bodies, to understand the financial status and progress of the organization. The ability to present these financial findings clearly, concisely, and accurately is essential for informed decision-making.

Financial analysis is another key area of responsibility. This involves a deep dive into the financial data to identify trends, risks, and opportunities. The Aviation Finance Manager then provides strategic insights that inform the organization's decision-making processes. This could involve analyzing the profitability of different routes in an airline, assessing the financial viability of fleet expansion, or identifying cost-saving measures.

The skills required for an Aviation Finance Manager are specialized and extensive. As mentioned, financial acumen is at the core of this role, encompassing a comprehensive understanding of financial principles and practices. This knowledge is critical in accurately managing and reporting on the organization's financial status.

Analytical skills are equally important. The ability to analyze complex financial data and extract meaningful insights is crucial for guiding the organization's financial strategy. This involves not only a keen eye for detail, but also the ability to understand broader market trends and economic factors that could impact the organization.

Moreover, the capacity to make strategic financial decisions is a key skill for an Aviation Finance Manager. This involves weighing various financial options, considering both risks and potential benefits, and making decisions that align with the organization's long-term objectives. It's a role that requires a balance between caution and ambition, ensuring that the organization's financial strategies support sustainable growth and success.

In essence, the Aviation Finance Manager is a key figure in steering aviation organizations towards financial stability and growth. Their role involves a blend of meticulous financial management, insightful analysis, and strategic decision-making, making them integral to the success of any aviation organization.

Aviation Sales and Marketing Manager

This position involves a strategic blend of marketing insight, industry knowledge, and creativity, aimed at boosting the organization's market presence, attracting customers, and ultimately contributing to its growth.

One of the core responsibilities of an Aviation Sales and Marketing Manager is the development and implementation of effective marketing strategies. This involves identifying the target market and understanding their needs, preferences, and behaviors. The manager must craft marketing campaigns that resonate with this audience, effectively communicating the value and benefits of the aviation services offered. This process often involves a mix of traditional and digital marketing techniques, including advertising, public relations, social media outreach, and event marketing.

In addition to creating marketing strategies, this role also encompasses the management and execution of these campaigns. This means overseeing the creative process, from concept development to content creation and campaign launch. The manager must ensure that all marketing efforts are cohesive, consistent with the brand's image and messaging, and effectively reach the intended audience.

Aircraft Fleet Manager

Fleet Managers take care of the logistics of maintaining a fleet of aircraft so that companies that rely on aircraft transportation in their business can remove or minimize the risks associated with aircraft investment, improving efficiency and productivity.

One of the primary duties of a fleet manager is organizing aircraft repairs. This involves not only identifying when repairs are needed but also ensuring they are carried out promptly and to the highest standards. The fleet manager must coordinate with maintenance teams and service providers, overseeing the repair process to minimize downtime and ensure the aircraft are returned to service as quickly and safely as possible.

Scheduling routine aircraft maintenance is another critical responsibility. Regular maintenance is essential for the safety and reliability of the fleet. The fleet manager must develop and adhere to a comprehensive maintenance schedule, ensuring each aircraft receives the necessary checks, servicing, and preventive care. This task requires a keen understanding of the maintenance needs of different aircraft types and the ability to plan maintenance activities in a way that optimizes fleet availability.

Overseeing the financial aspects of aircraft is also a key part of the Fleet Manager's role. This includes managing budgets, controlling costs, and ensuring the financial viability of the fleet operations. The Fleet Manager must track expenses, from maintenance costs to crew salaries, and make informed financial decisions to maintain the profitability of the fleet.

Tracking and diagnosing aircraft functions are crucial for ensuring operational efficiency and safety. The fleet manager uses various tools and technologies to monitor the performance and condition of each aircraft. This data is vital for identifying potential issues before they become major problems and for planning maintenance and repairs effectively.

Managing aircraft crew members is an important human resources aspect of the role. The fleet manager is responsible for coordinating crew schedules, ensuring adequate staffing for all flights, and managing training and certification requirements. They must ensure that crew members are qualified, well-trained, and ready to provide safe and efficient service.

Booking private jet or helicopter charters is another service that may fall under the purview of a fleet manager. This involves coordinating with clients to understand their travel needs, scheduling aircraft and crew, and ensuring that all aspects of the charter service meet the client's expectations.

Managing fuel consumption and costs is vital for both the economic and environmental efficiency of the fleet. The fleet manager must implement strategies to optimize fuel use, negotiate with fuel suppliers, and monitor fuel prices and consumption patterns.

Implementing health and safety programs is essential in an industry where safety is paramount. The fleet manager is responsible for ensuring that all operations comply with health and safety regulations, developing safety protocols, and conducting regular safety training for staff.

Facilitating partnerships between aircraft operators and clients/passengers is a key aspect of customer service and business development. The fleet manager acts as a liaison, ensuring that the needs and expectations of both parties are met, and fostering positive relationships that benefit both the operator and the client.

Lastly, adhering to the regulations of the Federal Aviation Administration (FAA) is a critical legal responsibility. The fleet manager must ensure that all operations comply with FAA regulations and guidelines. This includes staying updated on regulatory changes, maintaining necessary certifications, and ensuring that all aspects of the operation, from aircraft maintenance to crew training, meet the required standards.

Aviation Training Manager

An Aviation Training Manager's primary responsibility is to oversee the training programs for all aviation personnel. This includes pilots, cabin crew, ground staff, maintenance technicians, and any other staff whose roles directly impact aviation operations. The manager must ensure that these training programs are comprehensive, up-to-date, and effectively equip staff with the necessary skills and knowledge. This involves not only developing and updating training materials but also determining the best methodologies and technologies to facilitate learning.

Ensuring compliance with regulatory requirements is a critical aspect of the role. As we've mentioned previously in this book, aviation is a highly regulated industry with stringent standards set by authorities like the Federal Aviation Administration (FAA) and the International Civil Aviation Organization (ICAO). The Aviation Training Manager must have an in-depth understanding of these regulations and ensure that all training programs meet or exceed these standards. This compliance is crucial for maintaining the certifications of the personnel and the operational licenses of the aviation company.

Improving training effectiveness is another key responsibility. The Aviation Training Manager must continuously evaluate the effectiveness of training programs and seek ways to enhance them. This might involve incorporating new training technologies, such as simulators or e-learning platforms, or updating the curriculum to reflect changes in the industry and technology. The goal is to ensure that the training is not only compliant with regulations but also relevant and effective in equipping aviation personnel with the skills needed in a rapidly evolving industry.

In terms of skills, training and development expertise is fundamental. An Aviation Training Manager must be well-versed in adult learning principles, instructional design, and the latest training methodologies. This expertise enables them to design and implement training programs that are engaging, effective, and conducive to learning.

Knowledge of aviation regulations is equally critical. The manager needs to be up to date with current regulations and understand how they apply to various aspects of aviation operations. This knowledge ensures that training programs not only comply with legal requirements but also prepare personnel to operate safely and effectively within the regulatory framework.

Communication skills are also vital for an Aviation Training Manager. They must be able to communicate clearly and effectively with a diverse range of people, from trainees to regulatory bodies, and other stakeholders. This involves not just conveying information but also listening and responding to feedback, which is essential for the continuous improvement of the training programs.

Airline Customer Service Manager

The role of an Airline Customer Service Manager is integral to the airline industry, where customer satisfaction is a crucial determinant of success. This position involves a comprehensive approach to managing customer service operations, addressing passenger concerns, and fostering a positive experience for every customer.

At the core of an Airline Customer Service Manager's responsibilities is the management of all aspects of customer service operations. This includes overseeing the day-to-day activities at check-in counters, gate services, and lounge facilities, ensuring that each touchpoint in the customer's journey is smooth, efficient, and pleasant. The manager coordinates the efforts of customer service teams, ensuring they deliver high-quality service that aligns with the airline's standards and values.

A significant part of their role involves resolving passenger issues. Travel can be fraught with unpredictability, from flight delays and cancellations to baggage mishaps and booking concerns. The Customer Service Manager must adeptly handle these issues, providing timely and effective solutions that address passengers' needs and concerns. This not only involves direct interaction with passengers, but also coordinating with other departments, such as baggage handling, flight operations, and reservations.

Ensuring a positive customer experience is the overarching goal of an Airline Customer Service Manager. This means going beyond just addressing problems. It involves proactively seeking ways to enhance the customer experience, whether through improved service protocols, personalized services, or responding to feedback and suggestions from passengers. The manager plays a crucial role in shaping the airline's customer service policies and practices, always with an eye towards elevating the overall customer experience.

In terms of skills, a customer service orientation is paramount. An Airline Customer Service Manager must have a genuine desire to help and please customers, coupled with an understanding of what constitutes excellent customer service in the airline industry. This orientation helps in making decisions and implementing strategies that prioritize the customer's needs and satisfaction.

Last Thoughts

These career options within aviation management cater to individuals with diverse skills and interests, from operations and safety to finance and marketing. The specific path you choose will depend on your strengths, preferences, and career goals within the aviation industry. What is certain, is that each position is highly demanding, but also highly rewarding. Any career you choose will likely be a great choice.

Above everything else, aviation management involves the management of people—people who jump for joy when things go well, and blow a gasket when things go poorly. It's a difficult position to be in, primarily because so much rides on the people in these roles to perform at a high level of efficiency.

While it can be a stressful job at times, the one aspect of aviation management that I personally love is the ability to put a smile on a person's face when they know that they are understood OR when I can look a passenger in the eye and see their stress level go down when I assure them, they will be alright.

Chapter 11:
How To Find A Job In Aviation

Now you have reviewed all the different positions in the aviation industry, the primary question becomes: how in the world do I get one of these amazing jobs?

Well, the aviation recruitment process can vary depending on the specific position and the company involved. However, there are common elements and stages that are typically part of the hiring process in the aviation industry, but there are some elements that are common though all aviation application process which include the following steps.

Step 1: The Application Submission which are usually done online. Most aviation job openings start with candidates submitting their applications online through the company's career portal or job board. This usually involves uploading a resume and, in some cases, a cover letter.

Step 2: The Initial Review: Aviation Recruiters or hiring managers review submitted resumes to assess whether candidates meet the basic qualifications for the position. This may include relevant education, experience, certifications, and skills.

Step 3: Communication with Recruiters: Shortlisted candidates may be contacted for an initial phone interview or screening. This conversation helps recruiters to further assess the candidate's qualifications, motivations, and general fit for the role.
Assessment Tests:

Step 4: Technical and Aptitude Tests: Candidates may be required to take technical or aptitude tests to evaluate their skills and knowledge relevant to the job. Pilots, mechanics, and other technical roles may undergo specific assessments.

Step 5: Panel or One-on-One Interviews: Successful candidates from earlier stages are usually invited for in-person or virtual interviews. These interviews may involve discussions with HR, hiring managers, and sometimes technical experts. Behavioral questions and technical assessments may be included.

Step 6: Verification of Credentials: Once a candidate is identified as a potential hire, background checks are conducted to verify education, employment history, certifications, and other relevant credentials.

Step 7: Physical and Health Assessments: Certain positions, especially those involving flight operations, may require candidates to undergo thorough medical examinations to ensure they meet health and fitness standards.

Step 8: Contacting Previous Employers: Hiring managers may contact the candidate's previous employers to gather insights into the candidate's work performance, reliability, and professionalism.

Step 9: Offer Negotiation: Upon successful completion of the previous stages, the company extends a job offer. This may involve negotiations on salary, benefits, and other terms of employment.
Onboarding:

Orientation and Training: Once the candidate accepts the offer, they go through an onboarding process, which includes orientation, training, and introduction to the company's policies and procedures.

It's important for candidates to research the specific hiring process of the company they are applying to, as it can vary. Additionally, networking within the industry and staying updated on industry trends can be beneficial for securing aviation-related positions. For technical roles, possessing the necessary certifications and maintaining a strong safety record is often crucial.

The Importance of Being STEM-Minded. Role of Analytical and Problem-Solving Skills in Aviation.

As a child, did you ever look up at an aircraft flying above you and ever wondered how a machine that weights thousands of tons can appear to defy the laws of gravity, pulling itself off the ground with its powerful engines, into the sky?

There are many laws of physics and mathematics involved to make this process happen. This is the study of STEM (Science, Technology, Engineering, and Mathematics).

The aviation industry stands as a remarkable testament to the prowess of STEM. This sector is not just about aircraft soaring in the skies; it's a complex amalgamation of engineering marvels, operational logistics, and stringent safety protocols, all of which are steeped in the principles of STEM.

At the very heart of aviation lies science. It's not just the physics of how airplanes defy gravity - it's also the atmospheric science that pilots use to understand and predict weather patterns. It's the acoustics in aircraft design that make cabins quieter, and it's the chemistry in developing more efficient and less polluting fuels. Every aspect of flight, from the thrust of engines to the reduction of drag, is a science in its own right.

Along with science, another vital aspect of aviation is mathematics. It's present in the flight trajectories, fuel calculations, load balancing, and in the algorithms that manage air traffic. Pilots use mathematics to calculate speed, distance, and time, while air traffic controllers use it to keep skies safe. Mathematics is also crucial in financial and operational aspects, from determining flight schedules to optimizing routes for cost-efficiency.

Every flight is a culmination of scientific knowledge, technological innovation, engineering prowess, and mathematical precision. As we continue to witness advancements in this field, the role of STEM in driving these innovations becomes increasingly evident, highlighting the industry's reliance on a skilled, STEM-minded workforce.

The Balance of Left Brained and Right Brained Thinking in Aviation

Do you consider yourself "right brained" or "left brained"? Do you tend to analyze, rely on logic, and pay attention to details? Or are you highly imaginative, tend to doodle and often lose track of time?

We live in a society, for the most part, that favors left brain thinking – logic, science, and practicality -- over the right-brained artistic types who are generally viewed as less successful, productive or capable, none of which is true, but the type of cast, nonetheless.

The truth is that when you can balance right and left-brain tendencies, you are better able to problem solve, be productive, be creative and ultimately, less stressed.

The short answer is yes, it is important to have a strong understanding of physics and math to become a pilot and many other roles in the aviation industry.

A friend of mine, a Dutch pilot told me that flying an airplane is all about Mathematics and Physics. Just think about it for a second, how is an airplane able to take off with all that weight? How does lift and drag work and how do you calculate the top of descent or distance an airplane needs to fly in order to maintain a 3-degree glide path to the runway?

Profiles of Successful Aviators and Their Educational Backgrounds

Probably the most famous female pilot is Amelia Earhart. She is known as a pioneer in piloting and was the first female pilot to fly solo across the Atlantic Ocean. Earhart's determination to pursue flying was met with financial and societal challenges, but she persisted. She took various jobs, including as a truck driver and stenographer, to save for flying lessons. She bought her first plane, a second-hand Kinner Airster, in 1921 and quickly began to set records, including reaching an altitude of 14,000 feet in 1922, a record for female pilots at the time.

Earhart's final and most ambitious flight was an attempt to circumnavigate the globe in 1937. Along with her navigator, Fred Noonan, she embarked on the journey in a twin-engine Lockheed Electra. After completing more than two-thirds of the journey, Earhart and Noonan disappeared over the central Pacific near Howland Island under mysterious circumstances. Despite extensive search efforts, they were never found, and their disappearance remains one of the greatest unsolved mysteries of the 20th century.

The journey to become a pilot is not always an easy one.

Former flight attendant and newly certificated private pilot Kerri Beuker was no stranger to those traits, putting in just over two years of hard work in the metro-Chicago area to earn her wings. I sat down with Kerri to discuss her journey to become a pilot, including the various obstacles she faced and how she overcame them. I was inspired by her story and hope it will help educate and motivate others to embark and/or continue their journey to obtaining a pilot certificate.

Building a Strong Resume

It's probably been pounded into you that your resume is often the first point of contact between you and potential employers. In aviation, where precision and professionalism are paramount, your resume needs to reflect these qualities. A well-structured, clear, and concise resume sets the tone for your application, making a positive first impression that can land you in the interview seat. Here is how you can build a strong resume.

Here's how to make a resume in 10 steps:

Navigating the job market can be challenging, but having a stellar resume is key to getting noticed. A well-crafted resume can open doors to exciting career opportunities.

1. Pick a Resume Layout
Start by selecting a layout for your resume. The layout should be professional and easy to read. Consider using a chronological, functional,

or combination format based on your career history and the job you're applying for.

2. List Your Contact Information
At the top of your resume, include your name, phone number, email address, and LinkedIn profile. Make sure this information is up-to-date and professional.

3. Summarize Your Value as a Professional in an Introduction
Craft a brief introduction or summary that highlights your professional strengths, key accomplishments, and the value you bring. This section should be a snapshot of your best professional self.

4. List Your Work Experience and Accomplishments
Detail your work history, focusing on roles relevant to the position you're applying for. For each job, list your title, the company's name, dates of employment, and bullet points of key achievements and responsibilities.

5. Showcase Your Skills
Identify the skills that are most relevant to the job. This can include technical skills, soft skills, and languages. Be specific and honest about your level of expertise in each area.

6. Highlight Your Education
Include details about your educational background. List your degrees, the institutions where you studied, and any relevant honors or achievements.

7. Add Other Sections That Strengthen Your Resume
Consider including additional sections such as certifications, volunteer work, publications, or professional affiliations. These can provide a more comprehensive picture of your abilities and interests.

8. Choose a Design for Your Resume
Select a design that is clean, professional, and appropriate for your industry. Avoid overly complicated designs that can distract from the content.

9. Proofread Your Application

Carefully proofread your resume to eliminate any typos or grammatical errors. Consider asking a friend or mentor to review it as well.

10. Email Your Resume

Finally, when you're ready to apply, tailor your resume to each job application. While this may seem like common sense, it's surprising how many applicants fail in these small details. Use a professional email address, write a concise and compelling email body, and attach your resume in a compatible format.

Evaluating Problems and Opportunities in Aviation

As mentioned a few times in this book, the COVID-19 pandemic has hampered the airline industry and it's ripple effect will be felt for many years to come. After the sector began to recover in 2021, new waves of the virus and new travel restrictions prevented expansion. In the first months of 2022, global passenger traffic (RPK) recovered to 50 percent of pre-pandemic levels, but intercontinental traffic has a long way to go.

Even beyond the massive disruptions caused by COVID-19, the air industry is poised for significant change. Threats for new pandemics, supply chain issues, staff shortages, decline in business travel, worries about global economy and geopolitical instability, are only a few points of concern. In addition, climate change policies regulatory updates, and technology advancements will likely lead to changes in the way the industry conducts its business.

The best place to see the problems and opportunities in aviation is to seek the perspective of ICAO. For that I think it is best to look at the future of Aviation from ICAO.

The Importance of Joining Professional Organizations

Professional organizations provide numerous opportunities for continuous learning and skill enhancement. IATA and AOPA, for instance, offer specialized training, workshops, and seminars that keep members abreast of the latest trends, technologies, and regulations in the aviation industry. These organizations can offer invaluable resources for individuals starting or advancing their careers in aviation.

These organizations can also open doors to a vast network of industry professionals which can lead to mentorship opportunities, job openings, and collaborations that might not be accessible otherwise.

For those new to the industry, mentorship is a critical component of professional growth. These organizations often have mentorship programs where seasoned professionals guide newcomers, offering advice and support as they navigate their careers.

I would highly recommend that along with your additional training, schooling, you go above and beyond by attending networking events and professional get togethers whenever possible. These experiences and the people you will meet will be invaluable in your career.

Chapter 12:
The Future Of Aviation

It is well known the aviation industry faced unprecedented challenges during the COVID-19 pandemic, with travel restrictions, lockdowns, and decreased passenger demand leading to massive losses for airlines. This led not only to layoffs, but many pilots, engineers, air traffic controllers, and other support staff to take early retirement, unable or unwilling to deal with the increased stress and pressure that was caused by the Pandemic. While some staff have been rehired, promoted, and shuffled around, there is still a gap, which is growing, between the filled positions and the growing demand.

While it may seem like the world has forgotten COVID and has gone back to the way things were, the aviation industry is still recovering. Thankfully for the aviation industry, new opportunities continue to emerge. For example, many airlines are now placing orders for new aircraft while preparing to retrain and onboard staff. This period of recovery and adaptation not only signals a resurgence in air travel but also presents an opportunity for airlines to modernize their fleets, ensuring a more efficient and sustainable future in aviation.

In this chapter, we'll discuss the future of aviation. While predicting is always a tricky business, there are some emerging trends that will likely shape the field. These changes will be, of course, technological, but there are other factors to consider which will heavily impact the industry.

Supersonic Aircraft Innovation

Nostalgia often takes us back to the golden age of air travel—a time when the journey was as glamorous as the destination. Passengers reminisced about the spacious seating, the gourmet meals, and the unique thrill of crossing the Atlantic Ocean. A symbol of those glory days was the Concord, which was able to make the trans-continental flight in under three hours.

Since the Concorde's retirement in 2003, the dream of rapid transatlantic travel seemed to fade. Recently, we have just accepted that it takes around 7 hours to go from New York to London. The focus has been on cutting costs, reducing ticket prices rather than the time it takes.

However, perhaps that can change: NASA is at the forefront of supersonic flight, suggesting that future New York-London flights could shrink to a mere 90 minutes. Perhaps one day it might be normal to travel from New York, work a full business day and then be back in New York. Similarly, one day a commercial flight could reach speeds up to Mach 4—over 3,000 miles per hour.

To this end, NASA has conducted studies indicating a market for such rapid services, pinpointing approximately 50 viable routes primarily over oceans to comply with current regulations that restrict overland supersonic travel in many countries, including the U.S.

NASA's initiative involves the development of the X-59 aircraft as part of the Quesst (Quiet Super Sonic Technology) mission, aiming to produce "quiet" supersonic aircraft that could potentially change the restrictive rules against faster-than-sound travel over land. The X-59 is undoubtedly a strange-looking airplane. It has a long, slender nose that takes up roughly half of the airplane's design. But perhaps the strangest of features is the pilots cannot look out the front of the cockpit and the wings are small compared to the rest of the airplane!

Designed to muffle the disruptive sonic boom to a gentle thump, the X-59 is now in advanced stages of development. Lockheed Martin had completed its construction and preparing for a series of ground and flight tests. NASA's vision extends beyond the aircraft itself, as it contracts industry leaders like Boeing and Northrop Grumman Aeronautics Systems to explore and design the future of high-speed air travel, encompassing not only the technicalities but also the broader implications for safety, efficiency, economy, and society.

If successful, NASA's X-59 is poised to pioneer a new chapter in aviation history. The goal is to gather sufficient data to influence U.S. regulatory standards by 2027, potentially ushering in a future where time and distance are compressed, and the globe becomes more interconnected than ever before.

AI Is ON Everybody's Lips

Just like many other industries, artificial intelligence (AI) is poised to revolutionize the way airlines and the entire industry operate. AI, with its ability to process vast amounts of data, make real-time decisions, and optimize complex systems, is set to bring about transformative changes in aircraft design, safety, maintenance, air traffic management, and passenger services.

Unless you've been living under a rock, you've most likely heard about the recent advancements in AI. In aviation AI will likely emerge as a game-changer, promising enhanced efficiency, safety, sustainability, and passenger experiences. This fusion of cutting-edge technology with the aviation sector holds the potential to reshape the industry, making it smarter, more adaptive, and better equipped to meet the demands of the future."

AI in the Cockpit

Just imagine a future where AI systems take on the critical functions of helping or co-piloting the aircraft, responding in real-time to an array of flight variables with superhuman precision. It may sound like science fiction, but perhaps one day, many years from now, it will become a possibility.

The advent of autonomous flight is nurtured by the development of sophisticated algorithms capable of handling the intricate ballet of take-offs, cruising, and landings. These systems are designed to navigate through complex airspaces, negotiate weather disturbances, and resolve in-flight anomalies, all while ensuring optimal performance and safety. The promise is enticing: a future where the prevalence of human error is significantly diminished, if not entirely eradicated.

AI could continuously learn and adapt, drawing from every flight to refine its decision-making processes. Unlike human pilots, who may encounter a particular emergency scenario once in a lifetime, AI systems could virtually experience millions of such events, learning from a vast database of flight simulations, historical data, and real-time global aviation networks.

However, if you are looking at becoming a pilot, don't be alarmed; we haven't been able to figure out autonomous driving yet—an industry that has far fewer practical and regulatory hurdles. In fact, it's fair to say that someone just starting out flight training will not have to worry about AI taking their jobs forty or fifty years in the future.

Technologically, while AI has made leaps and bounds, the development of an autonomous system that can replicate or surpass the judgments of an experienced pilot remains an extremely difficult task.

Beyond just the technical aspects, the regulatory landscape presents another layer of complexity. Aviation authorities worldwide operate on the principle of safety, and the certification of potential pilotless aircraft introduces new variables into an already intricate regulatory equation. Regulators must grapple with unprecedented questions of accountability and standards for AI decision-making, requiring an evaluation of what safety means in the context of autonomous flight. Therefore, AI companies will likely have to do many years of testing to prove to these regulatory bodies that AI-flown planes are indeed safe.

Lastly, the public's acceptance of AI pilots is not a given. Again, looking at autonomous automobiles and how slowly that technology has progressed. Airline passengers have deep-rooted trust in human skill and intuition—attributes not easily attributed to lines of code. The industry must address the psychological and emotional dimensions of passenger comfort with autonomous flight, ensuring that trust is built through transparency, education, and a proven track record. Many people get extreme anxiety during flight—something that, imaginably, will only worsen if actual people are not in control of the plane.

The integration of AI into the cockpit heralds a transformative era for aviation—a horizon with much potential, but with many challenges that must be navigated with caution and foresight. The journey to autonomous or semi-autonomous flight will be evolutionary, marked by gradual steps that build upon each success and learning from every setback. It is a path where technology, regulation, and human factors will come together, guiding us towards a destination where the skies are a testament to the harmonious blend of human ingenuity and artificial intelligence.

Revolutionizing Air Traffic Control with Artificial Intelligence

While autonomous flight is far off, one area AI might be useful is in the role of air traffic control. The increasingly congested airspaces present a challenge to maintaining efficiency and punctuality. Yet, within this challenge lies an opportunity for AI to transform our skies.

With the deployment of machine learning algorithms, these sophisticated systems are trained to discern patterns within the complexities of air traffic flows. They will be able to analyze a multitude of factors, from flight schedules and meteorological data to the nuanced ballet of aircraft ascending and descending at bustling airports and figure out the best way to operate airliners.

It will be able to predict peak periods and potential bottlenecks with greater accuracy. This foresight enables air traffic controllers to proactively adjust flight paths and altitudes, smoothing the ebb and flow of aerial traffic. The result is a dynamic, fluid management of the airspace, where holding patterns are reduced, and aircraft are routed on the most efficient trajectories, conserving both time and fuel.

Again, it's unlikely AI will completely take over a human's role in guiding the sky—at least in most of our lifetimes. Far more likely is it will help assist the human air traffic controller in making better and quicker decisions. In situations where minutes can equate to significant costs and environmental impact, the ability to minimize idling in the air or on the tarmac is invaluable.

AI's capacity to manage complex data sets extends to predictive maintenance and operational planning far beyond what any human could do. By anticipating the needs of the airspace and the resources required to meet them, air traffic control can evolve from a reactive service to a proactive one.

However, trust in the system's reliability and security must be established, ensuring that the algorithms are not only sophisticated but will not malfunction or be prone to cyber threats. In all likelihood, the human element will remain pivotal, at least for the foreseeable future, with controllers and pilots needing to understand and trust the AI's decisions, creating a collaborative environment where human expertise and machine intelligence operate together.

A New Era of Maintenance

In the near future, maintenance is likely one of the areas where we will have the most advancements. The ability of AI to analyze vast data streams from aircraft sensors and logs has given rise to predictive maintenance—a method that relies on data-driven insights to forecast potential system degradations or failures before they happen.

AI algorithms could delve into the historical and real-time operational data of aircraft components, learning from patterns of wear and anomalies to predict their future state. This predictive capacity allows maintenance teams to transition from scheduled maintenance routines, which often adhere to conservative safety margins, to a more precise, need-based maintenance schedule. Such a tailored approach ensures that parts are serviced or replaced exactly when needed, not before or after their optimal service period. This precision timing maximizes the utility of each component, extends the life span of aircraft parts, and reduces the occurrence of unscheduled repairs that can cause costly downtime and operational disruptions.

The ripple effects of this proactive maintenance philosophy are significant. By pre-empting failures and optimizing maintenance schedules, airlines can enhance the overall reliability of their fleet. Aircraft are grounded for shorter periods, ensuring higher availability for flight operations, which, in turn, leads to improved profitability. Moreover, by addressing maintenance needs promptly and accurately, the safety of flights is bolstered—a paramount concern for passengers and aircrew alike.

Resource conservation would be another advantage of AI-driven maintenance. By avoiding unnecessary maintenance actions, not only are costs saved, but the environmental footprint of maintenance operations is also reduced. Fewer parts are discarded prematurely, and the consumption of materials and energy is aligned more closely with actual needs rather than estimated cycles.

As aviation continues to advance, the integration of AI into maintenance practices will continue be integrated. In this future, AI will not replace the human experience but rather enhances it, equipping maintenance professionals with the insights needed to ensure that aircraft are as safe in the skies as humanly—and now, algorithmically—possible.

Enhancing Passenger Experience with Artificial Intelligence

This is another area where there will likely be a lot of change in the next ten to twenty years. AI will offer personalized travel itineraries that are not just about the destination but the journey itself. It sifts through vast data—past travel history, wait times, customer feedback—to craft itineraries that minimize layovers, recommend preferred seats, and even suggest optimal travel times to avoid congestion. This level of customization was once a feature of luxury travel; now, AI brings it within the reach of the casual traveller, democratizing comfort and convenience.

The enhancements extend beyond the digital realm, manifesting palpably as passengers' step into the airport. Here, AI transforms into a guide and assistant. Interactive kiosks and chatbots, powered by sophisticated AI algorithms, stand ready to answer queries, from the location of amenities to real-time flight updates. With AI gone will be the days of queuing for information or grappling with the uncertainty of travel disruptions—AI ensures that guidance is but a touch or a voice command away.

Virtual assistants, accessible through smartphones and airport screens, are becoming ever-present companions. They help navigate through the increasing complex mazes of modern airports, offer updates on flight changes, and can even translate foreign languages in real-time, breaking down the barriers that can make international travel daunting.

Biometric systems embody another stride in the passenger experience, harnessing AI to enhance security while expediting processes. And facial recognition software swiftly verifies identities, reducing the need for boarding passes and identification documents. This not only accelerates the security and boarding processes but also adds a layer of security, as AI-powered systems meticulously analyze biometric data to ensure that only verified passengers board the aircraft.

But the influence of AI extends far beyond what can be seen by the visitors. AI algorithms analyze customer preferences to adjust lighting, temperature, and even scent, creating an environment that soothes and accommodates. In-flight, AI personalizes entertainment offerings, curated meal choices based on dietary preferences, and even predicts when passengers might need a pillow or a snack.

Despite these advancements, the implementation of AI in enhancing passenger experience is a delicate balance between personalization and privacy. Trust in the technology's use of personal data is paramount, and the aviation industry must navigate this aspect with transparency and stringent data protection measures.

The Evolution and Impact of Drone Technology

While complete automated flights are far off, one piece of technology that isn't is Unmanned Aircraft Systems (UAS), commonly known as drones. They represent a significant technological leap in aviation history. Many modern drones have been developed for military purposes by offering a strategic advantage in surveillance and reconnaissance missions without risking human lives. Their capability for remote operation and precision quickly made them indispensable in defence contexts as seen in the Ukraine and Russian war.

However, the potential of drones extends far beyond military applications, paving the way for their adoption in civilian sectors. As drone technology advanced, their size, cost, and usability improved, making them accessible for a variety of civilian applications. Today, drones are revolutionizing fields such as agriculture, delivery services, and film, offering innovative solutions that were previously unattainable.

In agriculture, for instance, drones have transformed traditional farming methods. Equipped with advanced sensors and imaging technologies, these drones can monitor crop health, soil conditions, and water levels, providing farmers with critical data to enhance crop yield and reduce waste. This precision agriculture not only boosts efficiency but also contributes to sustainable farming practices.

The delivery service industry has also seen a significant shift with the integration of drones. E-commerce giants and logistics companies are exploring drone delivery to expedite shipping processes, especially for last-mile deliveries. Drones offer a faster, more energy-efficient, and often more cost-effective means of delivering goods, particularly in areas where traditional delivery methods face challenges.

Surveillance and monitoring have been revolutionized by drones as well. Law enforcement agencies use them for traffic control, crowd monitoring, and crime scene analysis. In disaster management, drones provide crucial real-time information, aiding in search and rescue operations and assessing damage in areas that are otherwise inaccessible.

While the expansion of drone usage brings numerous benefits, it also presents regulatory challenges. Balancing the advantages of drone technology with safety, privacy, and security concerns has been a focal point for regulators. The regulatory landscape for drones is evolving, with authorities developing frameworks to integrate drone safely into national airspace systems.

One of the primary concerns is ensuring that drones do not interfere with manned aircraft operations. Regulations also address privacy concerns, as drones equipped with cameras can easily capture personal data without consent. Furthermore, there are security implications, given the potential misuse of drones for illegal activities.

Despite these challenges, regulatory bodies worldwide are making progress in establishing comprehensive guidelines and systems for drone operations. Collaborations between governments, industry stakeholders, and technology experts are crucial in shaping a regulatory framework that supports innovation while ensuring safety and privacy.

The journey of drones from military tools to multifaceted civilian assets reflects the dynamic nature of aviation technology. As regulatory landscapes continue to evolve and technology advances, the potential applications of drones are bound to expand, further transforming industries and daily life. This trajectory of drones not only illustrates the rapid pace of technological innovation in aviation, but also underscores the need for adaptive and forward-thinking regulatory approaches to harness the full potential of these remarkable machines.

The Horizon of Aviation Employment in the AI Era

Despite the transformative impact of AI technology, the cockpit and control towers will continue to be domains where human expertise and judgement remains irreplaceable for the foreseeable future.

As you have learned by now, the aviation industry is characterized by its stringent regulatory environment and the robust presence of unions. These bodies serve as the guardians of safety standards and the advocates for the workforce. As technology encroaches upon traditional roles, these institutions will play a pivotal role in navigating the transition, ensuring that the integration of AI and drones does not come at the expense of employment but rather works within the established framework to improve the industry while protecting its workforce.

The industry may witness scenarios reminiscent of historical labor disputes where workforces rallied against the encroachment of computers and automation. The difference in aviation lies in the high stakes of safety and security, which serve as a bulwark against rapid, unchecked automation. Any technological transition will likely be measured, deliberate, and subject to intense scrutiny, with unions at the helm, safeguarding the interests of their members.

In this future landscape, training and education will become even more crucial. The workforce will need to adapt, upskilling to meet the demands of a transformed industry where AI and human expertise coalesce. Rather than a replacement, AI could represent an opportunity for diversification and growth in aviation careers.

As we look to the horizon, the integration of AI and drone technology in aviation heralds a time of transformation. It is a vista of opportunity tempered by the imperative to navigate the future thoughtfully, ensuring that the human element, which has been the heartbeat of aviation since its inception, continues to thrive alongside the march of progress.

Space Flight: The Next Cycle of Innovation

It's strange to think about, but humanity is on the verge of expanding beyond the blue skies into the black expanse of space, heralding a new cycle of exploration and innovation. The endeavor of space flight, once monopolized by superpower nations, is being redefined by the pioneering spirits of private entities like SpaceX, Blue Origin, and Virgin Galactic. These trailblazers are at the helm, steering us toward an era that mirrors the boundless realms of 'Star Trek'—where space is not a distant, cold void but a frontier brimming with endless possibilities.

The initiatives spearheaded by these companies are reinvigorating the space industry with the same spirit that once fuelled the golden age of aviation. They have reignited the collective imagination, presenting space as a domain not just for the scientific elite or the robotic emissary but for everyone. This democratization of space travel symbolizes a profound shift, akin to the transition from the exclusive transatlantic voyages of yesteryear to the inclusive international air travel of today.

At the center of this shift is a technological revolution marked by groundbreaking innovations. Reusable rockets, now being pioneered by SpaceX, have already begun to alter the economics of space launches, suggesting a future where space travel could be as routine as catching an international flight from Hong Kong to New York. The implications of such advancements extend beyond space tourism, asteroid mining, or even the dream of Martian colonies; they suppose a future where intercontinental trips could occur outside the bounds of Earth's atmosphere, dramatically reducing travel times.

This cycle of exploration and innovation, fuelled by the audacity of private space firms, does not circle in a vacuum. Each successful launch and each milestone achieved resonates back to Earth, inspiring technological leaps that cascade into everyday life. The ripples of space exploration are felt in numerous terrestrial domains, propelling advancements in materials science, telecommunications, and even ecological stewardship, as we strive to understand and protect our home planet better.

The vision painted by these space pioneers is one of not just exploration but of a shared human destiny in the stars. Blue Origin's concept of millions living and working in space is not a mere fantasy but a tangible goal, driving the development of habitats and life support systems that could one day cradle human civilizations beyond Earth. Virgin Galactic's suborbital flights are poised to offer a glimpse of the astronaut experience to the public, democratizing the sense of awe and unity that comes from viewing our planet from above.

Yet the path to this stellar future is as challenging as it is thrilling. The physical risks of space travel, the environmental considerations of frequent launches, and the need for a new regulatory framework are all hurdles that must be surmounted with care and global cooperation. The stewardship of this next frontier demands a confluence of innovation, regulation, and ethical consideration, ensuring that the expansion into space is responsible and sustainable.

Made in the USA
Columbia, SC
21 June 2024